FACING GRIEF

bereavement and the young adult

Susan Wallbank

THE LUTTERWORTH PRESS
CAMBRIDGE

The Lutterworth Press
P.O. Box 60
Cambridge
CB1 2NT

www.lutterworth.com
publishing@lutterworth.com

ISBN 0 7188 2807 0

British Library Cataloguing in Publication Data
A catalogue record is available from the British Library

Printed in the United Kingdom by
MFP Print

CONTENTS

INTRODUCTION

Our society has been described as one which worships youth: and the qualities we value most are those associated with being young - energy, enthusiasm, fitness, beauty and hope. Youth implies birth and creation. We do not associate the young with loss and death. And why should the young want or need to think about such subjects? For them, death lies a long way ahead. Surely they should be concentrating on the creation of new beginnings, and leave the endings to those closer to them? Sadly, the young are not immune to death and bereavement simply because of their age.

Statistics from the Population Concenses and Surveys show that in the United Kingdom around 650,000 people die each year. 1,500,000 people will suffer a major bereavement because of those deaths. Of those 650,000 annual deaths, approximately 15,000 will be young people under the age of twenty. Each day in Britain approximately 500 wives will become widows and 120 husbands become widowers. Every year, 180,000 children under the age of 16 are growing up in families where either their mother or their father has died.

Although 90 per cent of all deaths in the United Kingdom will occur in those over the age of sixty, it is impossible for the young to remain untouched by these facts of death:-

An old man dies and a young person loses a grandfather.

A middle aged woman dies and a young person loses a mother.

A child dies and a brother or sister is lost.

An infant dies and young parents lose their baby.

Because we are young we do not expect to have to face the death of those we love. This may mean we will be unprepared, practically and emotionally, for these often unexpected, and untimely endings.

Our first experience of death and bereavement is likely to have a profound effect on us, and on the way we view life.

A Decade Of Change

Young adulthood has no clear boundaries. It exists somewhere between eighteen and twenty eight.

It is within this decade that most of us leave our parent's home and set up in a place of our own. Universities and colleges of higher education will take some young people away from the family home, whilst others will be starting paid employment and discovering the world of the working week and monthly pay slip.

This is a period for creating new partnerships; for meeting and falling in love, and perhaps getting married. Inside these new partnerships new families are created as children are conceived and born. Few decades in our life hold the potential for such great change.

New Titles and Positions

These practical changes in how we live are reflected in the new titles and positions we begin to acquire. From being a school child and a son, or daughter, we may rapidly move on to newly-defined identities. To becoming a student, a worker, a home owner, an aunt or uncle, a husband or wife, and possibly, a mother or a father.

Not only do we feel different because of the changes in our life but we soon discover that we are treated differently by those around us. More is expected from us - and our expectations of what others will do for us is modified. As a child we assume we will be fed, cared for and supported by other people. As an adult we take upon ourselves the responsibility for these tasks.

We may have a home to care for and other people relying on us to support them. If we have children, we, ourselves, become parents; so completing the circle of development. We are the head of the unit now. It belongs to us, not we to it.

Just because we move away from our parents home and take on new responsibilities, it does not mean that we cease to be our parents' child. We remain that for as long as we live, but our allegiance to our first family will be challenged by the fact that we now belong to a new group, and that group now has a claim on our time and energy.

For many this process is a complicated and difficult one. The path ahead is rarely straightforward. The years which contain our late teens and twenties are often ones of experiment. We often seem to take one step forward and two back again. It is a time for falling in and out of love. A time of acute excitement or stultifying boredom. For each new beginning there is always an ending. For each gain there can be an accompanying awareness of things lost.

Death - The Ultimate Ending

It is in this period of changing roles, of endings and new beginnings, that death may strike - and death is the ultimate, all time, forever ending.

No one can live long without confronting the prospect of death. Examples of it appear daily on television, in films and books and newspapers. The fear of death hangs like a terrible cloud above our heads; with the very future of the world threatened by man's misuse of his environment. We are surrounded by the possibility of death. We breath it in when we smoke another cigarette. We challenge it when we have that second drink or are not quite careful enough when driving or crossing the road. The coming of Aids has cast a threatening shadow over love-making and sexual relationships.

We may think we are used to living close to death, but we are not. A death in our late teens or twenties is likely to be our first close experience of death and bereavement. It can touch us in a way that we could never have believed possible; we find ourselves having to use unfamiliar words to describe our new identity - I am bereaved, and I am grieving.

If, in our past, we have experienced the death of someone close to us, then a major change in our life, such as another death, can bring that previous loss back into focus. For a while we may find ourselves grieving the past-bereavement alongside the present one.

Theoretical loss is very different from the actual loss of someone we love - someone who is, or has been, an important part of our life.

Besides the practical and emotional affects such a loss has upon us, it is through personal bereavement that we come face to face with our own mortality and the true vulnerability of all human beings.

The Rules of Bereavement
How long does grief last? Are such feelings normal? Why aren't I feeling anything? Am I going mad? Indeed, are there any 'rules' of bereavement?

There may be no-one around to answer our questions and it is not easy to find clear information on the subject of grief.

Death may not be the taboo subject it was a few years ago but it is something most people would still prefer *not* to think or speak about.

It isn't easy to know what to say to someone who has just lost someone they care for deeply. It often seems much safer to say nothing; to pretend that things are just the same and that nothing of any importance has happened.

The Importance of Loss by Death
Something of major importance has happened. Something so important that life can never be quite the same again. The death of a sister or father, a mother or a close relative, a lover or a wife, a baby, a little child or a close friend will change, not just the pattern of our life but, how we see ourselves and others, and how we perceive the world around us.

It is not a question of *recovering from* or *getting over* a major bereavement. There can be no recovery from such an event. Death is not like an illness, it is closer to an amputation. We have to learn life anew, without the person we have lost being there as part of it.

In that process of learning we will ourselves be changed. We will develop sensibilities and skills that would not have been part of our experience if we had not been bereaved.

THE BUSINESS OF DEATH

THE PRACTICAL BUSINESS OF DEATH

If we are the next of kin, or closely related to the one who has died, we will quickly discover that the death cannot remain our personal and private loss. A death sets in motion a chain of events which can involve the skilled intervention of many different professional people.

The Cast.(not necessarily in order of appearance)

The **POLICE** will have a duty to investigate the events leading up to and surrounding all sudden and unexpected deaths.

The Police may also have the difficult job of having to break the news of a death to relatives of the deceased.

A **DOCTOR** must certify that the person is dead. They will issue a medical certificate of cause of death if this is known.

A **POST MORTEM** will be requested if the causes of death are unclear.

The **REGISTRAR** will register the death and issue a disposal certificate (which allows the body to be buried or cremated) and death certificates.

The **CORONER** will be notified when the death needs to be investigated because it has happened suddenly or because it is not clear how or why it happened. He may order an Inquest.

An **INQUEST** is a court presided over by the coroner. It's function is to investigate the circumstances surrounding the death and determine the cause of death.

The **FUNERAL DIRECTOR** will arrange with the next of kin all matters concerning the cremation or burial of the body.

A **MINISTER OF RELIGION** may be asked to hold the funeral service.

A **SOLICITOR** may be needed to help in the settling of the estate.

When death is a result of natural causes, then the business surrounding it may be completed in one or two weeks. If the circumstances leading to the death require investigation, then it may be many months before the results of the inquest are determined. It can be very hard indeed for the bereaved when there are such long delays.

THE PERSONAL BUSINESS OF DEATH

The death of someone close to us may force us to step suddenly into that unknown world of hospitals and crematoriums, of funerals and memorials.

We may be asked to make decisions on matters of which we have no previous experience or knowledge.

"May we do a post-mortem on the body?"

"Would you be prepared for organs of the body to be donated to someone in need of them?"

"Do you wish to view the body?"

"Do you want the body to be buried or cremated?"

Few situations in life demand such major decisions to be taken with so little preparation, and in such a short space of time.

May We Do a Post Mortem?

Where the death is unexpected or the causes of death is unknown, a post mortem examination of the body will be ordered by the authorities; and this, by law, has to take place.

There may be other cases where the hospital asks the next-of-kin for permission to hold a post mortem even though it is not essential.

In this case, the next of kin has the right to say if they object. The thought of a stranger cutting into the body of the one we love can be a deeply disturbing one.

Before refusing, it might be worth talking with someone from the hospital to find out why they are asking for this examination. It is possible that the information they might gain would help us have a better understanding of the cause of the death; as well as help them to help others at a future date.

They will be able to tell us how their examination might affect the body visually for those that wish to view it at a later date.

May We Use The Organs From The Body?

The next of kin may be asked for permission to use various parts and organs from the body so that others may be given an opportunity to live a better or longer life.

The person who has died may have had strong views on this subject, which can be used as the basis for a decision. However, it is not easy to be suddenly confronted with the necessity of making such a major decision knowing very little about what this might entail.

If large organs such as the heart and lungs are to be removed then usually someone from the hospital will be able to explain when and how this will be done. The fact that the body may be technically alive whilst being *brain-stem dead* needs careful explanation. Many relatives need to be assured that they are not depriving the one they love of any chance of life, however small this might be.

There can be great comfort in the thought that the tragic death of someone we love may give another person the opportunity to live a longer or better life.

Viewing The Body

We may have no choice as to whether or not we see the dead person. We may have been with them when they died, or, as a close relative, we may be asked to view the body in order that a positive identification can be made.

If this is not the case, then we can decide whether or not we wish to see the person we have lost.

Some people have no wish at all to view the body. They prefer the last memory of the person they have lost to be a living one - perhaps a smile, or the wave of a hand as they left the hospital ward. These images are important to them, and they do not want them disturbed by what might be less pleasant ones.

Others feel equally strongly that they must see the body. That, until they have done so, they will not be able to accept the death and they will not have completed their duty to the deceased.

In between these two definite positions is the less clear ground occupied by those who feel that - Yes, they ought, or want to see the body but perhaps they shouldn't because it might upset them, give them nightmares, or leave them with distressing and disturbing memories.

If the death has been a violent one there might be justifiable reservations.

The Funeral Director will be able to advise on the state of the body, and usually everything is done to make sure that any damage is minimised visually. If parts of the body are to be donated, surgeons are careful to ensure that the body is presentable afterwards.

The majority of people in Britain will die in hospital. We may be there when they die or, if we arrive soon after the death, we may be invited to view the body which may still be lying in a curtained off part of the ward or have been moved to a side ward or chapel of rest.

It is possible to arrange to have the body brought home to lie in the house until the funeral or cremation. In the past it was common practice that the body of the dead person was prepared at home and would remain there, watched over by members of the family until burial. It is more usual now a days for the body to be taken directly from home or hospital to the Funeral Director of our choice, where, after preparation it will remain, open to view, in one of their chapels of rest until the ceremony.

In some cultures it is exceptional for the body to be removed from the home before burial or cremation; in many countries the bodies of important people will be placed on open display in order that the public can pay their respects to the one who has died.

Some religions require very rapid burial of the body and this means there is less opportunity for relatives and friends to view it before burial.

Fear of The Unknown

As more deaths occur in hospital wards it becomes increasingly rare for us to see someone after their death. This can make the thought of seeing a dead body a little frightening because we do not know what to expect.

The majority of people who make the decision to view the body of someone they love, state afterwards that they are glad they chose to do so. Some find it comforting, although for others the experience is disturbing.

Confronting The Reality of Death

Seeing the body of the person we have lost, forces us to confront the reality of the fact that they are dead. It is much harder to deny the fact that the death has happened if we have actually seen the body and there is some evidence that doing so does help us face our loss.

The Funeral

The funeral ceremony plays an important part in how we grieve. It is a public acknowledgement of the death. Our private loss is placed alongside the loss of others who knew the deceased.

If we have the opportunity to attend the funeral we become part of the family and community group grieving the loss of the person who has died. The presence of the actual body at the ceremony, even enclosed in a casket or coffin, helps us to accept the reality of the death.

This public ceremony reflects the importance of the event that has just happened. In our society the dead are treated with dignity - as are those bereaved by that death.

What Kind of Funeral?

Most people in this country face a choice between burial and cremation and the majority today opt for cremation.

Our decision can be based on our religious faith. Some religions stipulate that the body must be dealt with in a certain way. Orthodox Jews and Muslims will not be cremated, whilst Hindus have a long tradition of cremation.

Our family circumstances will also influence our decision. If we have a family plot in a graveyard then this will be used in preference to cremation. The wishes of the deceased should be taken into consideration although there may be circumstances where these are best overridden, perhaps for practical reasons. The living also have rights at such a time and, as long as we do the best we can, there should be no guilt or anxiety if we decide not to follow instructions which may have been made without any real thought as to the difficulties they might bring about.

The cost of the alternative methods will also influence our choice. A burial can be more expensive than a cremation. It can involve purchasing a plot and buying and erecting a head stone. The continuing upkeep of the grave has also to be taken into account and weighed against the advantage of having that special place to visit.

Crematoriums offer a resting place for the remains of the deceased. The ashes can be scattered in the grounds and commemorated with a plaque or bush. Again, the cost of such optional extras should be carefully considered if financial resources are limited.

What Kind of Service?

Differing religious ceremonies will place different emphases on the meaning of the death. Some will highlight the loss here on earth whilst others will concentrate on the after-life and the joy that lies ahead. Most religions will accept that sadness is a justifiable emotion in those who are left behind on this earth.

If the deceased has no religious beliefs then it is possible to arrange a non-religious ceremony. The Humanist Society will help people arrange such ceremonies. It is sensible that such a decision be taken after consultation with all close family members. The funeral is an important occasion for many people.

The funeral service is a celebration of the life that has ended. A public acknowledgement of the importance of the person who has died, and of the contribution that they made to the lives of all those who are left behind.

If the Minister did not know the deceased he may ask relatives and friends for personal information that can be used in the service. Special music or songs that held particular significance for the deceased may be used in the ceremony.

Who Plans It?

Obviously the closer one is to the deceased the more rights one has in the planning of the occasion. Ultimately the responsibility rests with the next of kin, and their wishes should be respected. Unless the deceased has made a legal statement making someone their next of kin, it is assumed that the parents of an unmarried person will be next of kin. If the person is married then their husband or wife will automatically be next of kin.

Live-in partners have no automatic rights of kinship, whatever the length or significance of the relationship they shared with the deceased.

One of the first duties of those closest to the person who has died is to arrange for the news of the death to be circulated, first to family and friends and then to all others who will need to know. This breaking of bad news can be a deeply distressing experience and this is a time when kindness and support is most appreciated.

What if I Can't Get To The Funeral?

It is not always possible to attend the funeral of those we are close to. We may be away at the time, or circumstances outside our control prevent us from being there.

It is sad if we are not able to be part of this important occasion, but the fact that we are not there does not mean that our grieving process will be seriously affected. We may find that we need a little longer to take in the fact that the person has died. However, by sending flowers and a letter of condolence we can include ourselves, emotionally if not physically, in the funeral proceedings. Later on we can ask those who have attended it to tell us all about it.

It may be possible to ask the minister of our local parish to mention the loss we have suffered in a service taking place in the same week as the funeral.

What Happens After The Funeral?

After the funeral, families and close friends often gather together for a meal. This can prove to be a surprisingly relaxed occasion; a time for the sharing of good and pleasant, even humorous memories. Perhaps its main purpose is to re-enforce the closeness of the family and the group surrounding the one who has died.

A warning! Very powerful feelings are present at the time of the funeral. It is unfortunately not uncommon for rows to break out between family members or close friends.

The more complicated the family structure, the greater the likelihood someone will feel left-out or neglected in the funeral arrangements.

The etiquette surrounding this occasion has not moved with the times and there are no clear rules about inclusion of ex-wives or husbands or step family members.

Very often the root of the anger lies in our wish for recognition of the importance of our particular place in the life of the deceased.

What Is A Will?

A will is a written declaration of the deceased person's wishes on the distribution of his or her property after their death. It is a legal document and has the full backing of the law. If anyone feels they have a claim on the deceased's estate - everything that has been left by the person who has died - they can lodge an appeal against the will.

If there is no will, then the next-of-kin must apply to the probate registry for letters of administration. The estate will then be distributed according to the laws on inheritance.

The Very Personal Belongings

It is surprising how many personal belongings each of us accumulates as we travel though life: Toothbrush, medicines, shampoo, clothes, books, letters, bags and jewellery - the list can be endless.

If the person who has died lived alone then a whole household of objects may have to be sorted through, and those difficult decisions - to keep or not to keep - made almost immediately if the property has to be vacated.

If there is no deadline for clearance because the deceased owned their property or lived with us then this distressing work can be done at our own pace.

The letting-go of possessions reflects our ability to let go of the one we have lost. There are those who, in the first days of their bereavement, desperately search for that new start and this is expressed in the clearing out of every object that might act as a painful reminder of the past. At the other extreme there are the shrine-makers, those who, years after the death, cannot part with a single thing.

Just as emotionally, we are only able to let those we love go from our life a little at a time, so most of us allow the objects left behind by our loved ones, to pass from us in stages. There may be a first clearance, followed some months later by a second when we are able to claim a little more territory back from the dead. Some objects we may need to hold on to for a long time and there will always be those very precious things that will remain with us for the rest of our lives.

How Long Does It All Take?

It can take a long time for the business of death to be completed. It is not unusual for the process to still be at work a year after the death. Many are the complications and connections involved in a person's life - an annual subscription becomes due and the organisation has not heard that its member has died, another letter has to be written, another telephone call made.

Some computers seem to find it hard to accept the fact of death and persist in sending out bills and statements to the deceased no matter how many times they are informed of the change. Such reminders of the loss we have suffered can generate a feeling of anger at the world's seeming insensitivity.

GRIEF

"No one ever told me that grief felt so like fear."

These words, written by C. S. Lewis in his book *A Grief Observed* after the death of his wife, seem to sum up that sense of confusion and bewilderment so many people experience after the loss of someone they love. There are few situations in life for which we have less preparation than death and bereavement. It is highly likely that no-one will have told us that we might feel the way we do, or that our life will have been disturbed in the way that it has.

Grief is a complex process which we undertake in the weeks, months, and even years following the death of someone important to us. It encompasses a wide range of physical and emotional reactions, as slowly and painfully we attempt to adjust to life without that person.

Each of us will grieve in our own unique way for the unique loss that we have suffered. There is no right or wrong way to grieve. If we listen carefully to our own inner voice it will provide us with a very basic guide to what is best for us. It will tell us when we need to rest and when to exercise; when it would be better to talk things over, or best to remain silent. We will sense when we are becoming too inward-looking or when we are pushing ourselves too hard and fast.

Grief is immensely hard work. A major bereavement shatters the very structure on which our life is based. It will destroy many of the patterns, routines and assumptions that form the basis of how and why we think and act as we do. We will need to work out many of the daily actions we have been used to doing almost automatically. It is not until we lose our 'automatic pilot' that we realise just how much of our existence is under its control - without it, we find we quickly become exhausted. This learning to form a new set of routines is an often unrecognised part of the work of grief.

The fact that someone we know has died can be hard to take in. Reactions on hearing of a death can vary enormously.

DENIAL

"Dead, of course she's not dead. I only saw her yesterday. How can she be dead?"

"There must be some mistake. Someone else must have died."

Death is something that happens to other people not to us or to those that we love.

Our brain can refuse to accept information which appears so unbelievable and impossible - perhaps if we deny it enough, then it will make the death go away and everything will be all right once again.

Part of us knows that this is not possible. Even as we speak, the knowledge descends and we know deep inside that nothing is ever going to be the same again. The world has changed and it is not going to change back however much we cry or demand or scream or deny what has happened.

SHOCK AND NUMBNESS

Even if there is forewarning of death, it can still surprise and shock when it comes. The difference between life and death is so great, it is impossible to be totally prepared for it. With death there can be no tomorrow, no more hope, no opportunity to pass on that last message. Death draws a line between that which was and that which is, and there is no way we can cross over the gulf that exists between the past and the present.

Our inner world may have changed, but the world outside carries on much as it did before. We still get up in the morning; there are people to see, things to do, and life goes on in spite of what has happened.

It is not unusual for people to describe themselves as feeling like a robot in the early days of bereavement. This numbness can be disturbing.

"Shouldn't I be feeling something?"

"Why aren't I crying?"

The shock of the death can offer us a temporary protection which allows us the space to carry out the important business which follows a death. This is especially true if there are people relying on us to take charge or be in control of the situation. There isn't the time or the space for tears or emotions. Like automatons we do what we have to do. Sometimes a surge of emotion threatens to overwhelm us but it disappears and we go on.

The Physical Effects of Grief

The death of someone who is an important part of our life can affect us physically. We are used to thinking of feelings as being locked inside our head. We *think* we are unhappy. However, sadness and unhappiness can be experienced physically, as a gaping hole in the pit of our stomach, a tightness across the chest, as sickness, shaking, sweating hands, headaches and a hundred other symptoms. Many people find themselves sighing deeply in the early days of their bereavement. Our heart can actually have an ache around it.

It is also possible to experience the symptoms we might imagine the dead person would have felt when dying - a pain in the chest, breathlessness or a choking sensation. In time these symptoms pass away quite naturally.

A major bereavement can upset our sleeping and eating patterns. We become over-tired and irritable, we may lose weight or put it on if we eat for comfort. We may find that we cannot concentrate, think clearly or remember things after a bereavement. Shock underlies many of these early symptoms, and as it begins to fade so we begin to feel stronger.

SEARCHING

For days or even weeks after the death the borderline between belief and disbelief can be very finely drawn. We know the death has happened and yet find ourselves moving restlessly from room to room as if still searching for the person who has died. A stranger in the street suddenly becomes the one we have lost. We lay a place for them at the table, we still expect to hear their key in the door.

GHOSTS

It is not uncommon to feel the presence of the dead person. This need not be at all frightening. Some people say they hear a voice, perhaps whispering goodnight, others catch a glimpse out of the corner of their eye, or a particular smell hangs in the air.

Others describe a feeling of being somehow pulled after the dead person, as if being persuaded to join them in death. Such thoughts can be deeply disturbing. Many primitive peoples believe that the dead person's soul tries to return in the early days following the death - and perhaps remnants of these basic fears live on, deep inside all of us.

For the majority of people there is simply the sense that the person they have lost is nearby, watching over them and continuing to care for them. Usually these either comforting or disturbing feelings disappear after the first weeks of bereavement.

DREAMS AND NIGHTMARES

Dreaming of the one who has died can bring great comfort, and many tell of dreams where the person who has died visits them to offer reassurance that all is well.

Such dreams are very different from the nightmares that can also come during this period of high emotions and disturbed sleep. It is deeply distressing to wake out of sleep in the early hours of the morning, one's mind full of horrific images. The sense of threat and fear that such nightmares generate can last a long time.

It can be difficult, even in the safe light of day, to stand back from such dreams and nightmares and see them for what they really are - our mind's way of slowly working through the pain and distress of our bereavement. They are an expression of our inner struggle to find a way of coming to terms with the enormous loss we have suffered. As we move forward in our grief, so we leave these dreams and nightmares behind us.

Alternative Endings

Part of the intensely hard early work of grief is the need to explore the events leading up to, and surrounding, the death. In some ways this is rather like constructing a video which contains all the relevant details - the first signs of ill-health, the last time we saw the person alive, the things we were able to say, the things that were left unsaid.

This video is then played over and over again in our mind. Perhaps what we are really looking for is an alternative happy ending to our story. This is impossible, but we need to go on and on until the work is finished, and we are free to move forward once again.

The more complicated the manner of the death, the greater our need to try to understand the reason for it happening: The greater then, our search into those important final events.

Heroes and Villains

This is a time when we are most likely to feel either anger or guilt. Our mental video has to contain villains, someone who carries the blame for the tragedy. We may cast ourselves in that role, or there may be an obvious character just waiting to play the part. Our video might also possess its heroes, those that can do no wrong.

Sometimes we cast the dead person in this role and they become everything that is good. In reality, few people are completely perfect, or all bad - and as time passes we are usually able to see a more balanced picture.

ANGER

In the search to reach an understanding of the death and why it happened there will be times when we apportion blame. In doing so we may become angry.

"I am angry because if so and so had not taken that action then the death would not have happened and I would not be feeling as I do now."

There may seem to be an obvious instigator of the death; someone we can point to and accuse.

"You killed the person I love!"

In such cases we have justifiable anger. Our lives have been damaged for ever because of something another person has done.

What can we do with such justifiable anger? If society takes up our cause and punishes the wrong-doer then it may be easier for us to accept what has happened. If there is no just punishment then the burden falls on our shoulders to carry the cause forward. For if there is no public acknowledgement of the wrong done, it is hard for us to reach an acceptance of our loss.

We may also feel we have the right to justifiable anger even if the cause of the death was not so straight forward. Perhaps the loss happened through an act of neglect or carelessness, with no harm intended, but, through accident or circumstance, great harm was none the less done. We may feel obliged to act to ensure no others suffer through similar neglect - and, in so doing, channel our anger into action.

There can be a heavy price to pay in taking on such causes. They demand a large amount of energy at a time when we have very little of it. In order to find enough energy, we may need to generate anger, because anger is a great source of energy.

The rest of the hard work of grief is put to one side in the battle for revenge or justice. It is sometimes easier to fight than to think or to feel - and, when battles are lost, it is hard to avoid bitterness.

If our complaints are dismissed too lightly or not judged as important enough to pursue, we can become angry because we feel that those that should care do not care.

Such proper anger allows us to focus on the importance of what has happened; after all, this is our tragedy. A life has ended, one that mattered intensely to us, and it should be seen to matter to others as well.

Anger At Friends And Family

We may blame others in the family or close friends for the part they played, or failed to play, in caring for the one who has died. They too will be working through their grief. They too may be searching for their own understanding of the cause of the death. They too may be apportioning blame, and they too may be angry with themselves or with others. They may well have times when they are angry with us.

We may feel angry at our friend's and our family's failure to support us at this time when we most need their care and understanding. We may well feel let down by them.

Angry With God

We may find ourselves angry at our God for allowing such a thing to happen. Why did He ignore our prayers, let us down when we most needed Him?

It can be hard to reconcile the thoughts of a just and good God with the seemingly senseless suffering and death of someone who is very much loved and needed on this earth.

When we knew of the illness or accident we may have tried to strike a bargain with God - if He lets the one we love live, then we will do whatever is required in return. If the person dies, what then? Where do we go then, in our relationship with God?

Very often the death of someone we love forces us to re-assess our faith. This can be a very important part of the hard work of grief, as we struggle to come to terms with new understanding and a re-examined system of belief. Our religious community can also come under heavy attack at such a time. It too may appear to fail us: Our minister may not give us the help we need, our fellow worshippers ignore our painful feelings or fail to recognise what it is we want from them. We may not know ourselves what that might be, but we know that we are not getting it.

Anger At The World

Sometimes there is just pure anger. It doesn't seem to belong anywhere. There is no one to blame and no-one in particular we want to hurt. What happened has happened and nothing could have prevented it. We know that so well - and yet there is still anger hiding inside, waiting for a trigger to release it.

When we are feeling at our lowest, there is nothing which escapes our anger. The flowers that bloom seem to be deliberately provoking us by contrasting their colour and life with our sadness. The fact that the sun shines is an insult to the loss we have suffered.

We are angry at a world in which bad things happen to good people. Angry even, at the one who has died for being dead, for letting us down and abandoning us when we most need them.

Or we may not feel angry at all. The range of emotions is so wide after a major bereavement. All of us will experience different feelings. Each of us will grieve in our own way for the unique loss that we have suffered.

Anger At Ourselves

There is also anger we direct towards ourselves. Why didn't we see what was happening? Why didn't we say what we wanted to say? Why did we behave as we did? In looking for cause and effect we cannot dismiss our own actions. This is guilt - anger turned in upon ourselves.

It is possible that we have been guilty of neglect or selfishness or even worse. There may well have been times in the past when we actually wished the deceased dead - and the closer we were, the more likely this is to have been true.

GUILT: THE STARRING ROLE

Guilt places us at the centre of the picture. We might not like the role we have given ourselves, but at least it is a main part; a starring role.

We tell ourselves - if we had not done this or that, or if we had done such a thing, then the one we love would still be alive.

This is very different from recognising that in reality we are pretty powerless in the face of death. Whatever we did or said was really quite insignificant compared to a terminal illness or tragic accident, or even someone's personal decision to take their own life.

Guilt can be a way of clinging onto the idea that we are in control of everything in our world. To admit the fact that we are without the power to change events can be very frightening indeed.

Sometimes it is easier to feel guilt than to move on and begin to understand the full impact of what we have actually lost from our life for ever.

Guilt At Confrontation
Long-term relationships between people nearly always contain confrontation and anger as well as commitment and caring. It is impossible to live our lives as if they are about to come to an end at any moment. We seldom stop in mid-sentence - bite back the criticism - just in case they or we should die and we never get another chance to tell them that we really like them, even if we do disagree with them on some issues and this one in particular.

Guilt At What We Did Or Didn't Do
So often a death is not foreseen, and we are never given the opportunity of making amends. Death can come when we least expect it. Perhaps in the middle of a period of quarrelling and argument, which, if we were given time would have been resolved. But we have not been given time. There can be no resolution, no coming back together. This is intensely sad because we have been deprived of a proper ending and are left to cope with difficult and distressing emotions.

REGRET

Superficially regret and guilt seem remarkably similar. Both can be expressed through sentences beginning with the words,
"If only ..."

Both contain the wish that things should be different, that, if we had control over life events and could travel back in time, there would be things that we would change.

There are differences between guilt and regret. Often guilt is an inappropriate but inevitable temporary stage in the struggle to understand why a death has happened. Regret is a natural reaction to loss.

Because we can never do everything perfectly or anticipate the future there will always be a sense of regret when a life is cut short.

There may be regret over the death itself - that we will have to go on in this life for ever without the person at our side.

The loss of someone we care for deeply will leave us with such regrets. These may fade in time but they will always be there just below the surface of our life.

Memory

In the process of investigating the past we draw heavily upon our memory.

It is not unusual for the shock of hearing about the death to temporarily block out our ability to recall. In vain we search our minds for pictures of the deceased, we try and remember what they looked like or things they said but there is nothing there.

Alternately, our memory becomes distorted and we are only able to remember certain scenes - perhaps the bad times, or the pain of the illness.

As the shock fades it becomes easier to focus on the past and travel back in time. Having others around us prepared to talk over the past and remember parts of it with us can help. We may find that everyone's memories are distorted for a while, perhaps one person idealising the dead person and only remembering the good times; other recalling a very different picture of events. Eventually a more comprehensive, truthful picture emerges.

Major changes in our life can trigger memories which may have been hidden for many years. Loss can bring back long-forgotten earlier losses. Inevitably, this can increase our sadness for a while.

Forgetting And Remembering

When someone dies our concept of time can change. Normally we are conscious - if we think about it at all - of moving quite smoothly from out of the past and into the present, with the basic assumption that the future lies somewhere ahead of us in one form or another. A death destroys such assumptions. It draws a line across our life, clearly dividing that which occurred before our bereavement from that which happens after it. Little wonder our memory is disturbed.

CONTROL

Death is so often outside our control. It strikes when we least expect it. Even if there has been an illness and the end of life seems near, death can steal those we love away from us prematurely so that we have no chance to say that final goodbye. Death can come to those we love in the night when we sleep or when we have just slipped from the room for a much needed rest.

Yet when we wish for death to come and put an end to the pain and suffering of the one we love, then it stays away, day after day and month after month, refusing to bring release.

Nothing we do in our life can fully prepare us for the sense of helplessness we feel when confronted with the death of someone we love. Nothing we can do can bring back the dead. We are forced to accept the unacceptable.

The more we are the kind of person who thrives in a controlled environment, who is used to being seen as competent and in charge, then the greater our confusion and sense of bewilderment when we are bereaved and discover that whole areas of our life slip out of our control.

Sleep

So often sleep is disturbed in the early weeks and even months following a major bereavement. At the very time when we long for a good night's sleep, when we slip exhausted into bed and just want to drift away from the sadness and problems, sleep eludes us. We may drop off for a couple of hours, but find ourselves wide awake at two o'clock in the morning. Then, we lay there worrying until it is nearly time to get up and then fall into a deep sleep. The permutations of a bad night's sleep are endless.

Appetite

Normal, moderate patterns of eating can be much disturbed, especially in the difficult early days of grief. In a search for comfort, some people find themselves picking at food all day long. Others have no interest at all in eating; their stomach contracting into a tight ball at the mere thought of food.

Smoking And Drinking

When we are confused and hurting inside it is natural that we should turn to anything which gives us a little comfort or respite from the pain. Cigarettes and alcohol are a ready source of such help. Alcohol, which offers temporary relaxation is also, unfortunately, a depressant. It can bring us down into the kind of low which seems only curable by yet another drink. It is all too easy for a 'drinking habit' to be created, and with it a dependency on a drug which is hard to break - another way of finding ourselves and our lives becoming out of our control.

Tears

It is not unusual to cry a great deal. The fact that this is natural doesn't make it any easier when one finds oneself in floods of tears on a bus or in front of complete strangers in the supermarket.

Other people find that they cannot cry at all. They feel like crying, they can identify the sadness like an ache deep inside but it will not come out.

Both crying too much, or not crying at all, lead to a sense of being out of control of oneself and one's behaviour, and to the feeling that somehow one is not grieving properly. At such a time it is best to hold onto the fact that we can only grieve and express our grief in our own personal way.

FEARS AND PHOBIAS

The death of someone we love shocks and deeply disturbs us. It will force us to confront our own mortality and that of others that we love.

It is hardly surprising that we may be subject to high levels of fear. Everything in which we have placed our trust has been disturbed and will remain disturbed until we form a new basis of trust and regain confidence in life again.

Some people are frightened of death itself - either because death seems to offer only nothingness; or because life-after-death threatens pain or punishment.

In the very early days of bereavement there can be the primitive fear of being sucked towards death, perhaps even pulled there by the one we have lost. It may feel as if they are exerting an influence on us to follow them. Part of us may even be tempted to go with them; another part fighting to remain here.

Usually these dark feelings vanish quite naturally in a week or so, and it is possible that they stem from our pain in living on without that person, or from our guilt at still being alive and able to enjoy life.

We can fear for those we love; terrified that if we let them out of our sight they too may be lost to us for ever. Parents losing a child can fear for the safety of their other children; wanting to keep them close-by for a while. Children, losing a parent, can be desperately worried that their remaining parent might also die.

Our fear may focus itself in a wish to stay indoors. The home is seen as the only safe place, and the longer we stay within its walls the harder it can be to venture out again. Alternatively, there can be a constant, restless desire to get out into the open. Exhaustion soon affects those who find themselves tramping the streets or visiting relatives and friends day after day.

There can also be a fear that we are going out of control - fear that we are mad, or well on the way to becoming mad. The symptoms of extreme grief can be very close to the symptoms of mental illness, but there the similarities end. The vast majority of people do not go mad with grief and such distressing feelings do not last for ever.

Fear can exist simply as fear; a general sense of unease and threat hanging over us, from the moment we wake up in the morning to the point when we try to sleep again at night.

Fear is a natural component of bereavement. We may feel it only for a moment, or it may come and go for a week or so before disappearing. Sometimes it may remain with us for some time.

Help Against Fear

It helps to understand that fear is natural. It is important to hold onto the belief that we are not going mad, but reacting perfectly normally to one of the most demanding and distressing crisis situations we will ever be asked to undertake. By understanding this, we can at least, take away that fear of being afraid.

Sometimes, consciously trying to relax tensed up muscles can help and there are some excellent cassettes and books giving relaxation techniques.

If worried about a possibility of the fear turning into a more permanent phobic condition, then it is sensible to take action; perhaps by varying one's patterns of behaviour, or by seeking an outside opinion. A doctor will be able to offer advice on what, if any, medication it might be sensible to take.

PATTERNS OF GRIEF

Grief comes and goes, it flows in and out like the tide.

Even within the space of a day it is possible to see a pattern emerging in our grief. There will be a time in the day when the sadness seems greatest, and then times when it can be put to one side as the work of life goes on.

Then there are weekly patterns, particular days, perhaps the weekends, that begin to emerge as the 'bad' times.

As time passes it is possible to go a few days without feeling overwhelmed by the sadness. Then, down we go again and the pain seems to have doubled because now it is less expected and because we have grown to hope that we might just be over the worst.

There are high and low tides; some days we are strong and positive looking, other days we can only look back at the past and focus on the loss we have suffered.

Some tides are so powerful that it feels as if we might be swept away and carried far out to sea. However, we are in no real danger of drowning. Trying to swim against the tide and fight our way back to the shore is simply a waste of precious energy. Better to accept the validity of our own feelings, however sad and lost we may feel, and let ourselves drift - knowing that at such times we are engaged in the work of grief itself.

Sensible too, to accept the better times and not feel guilty that we have been allowed a moment of pleasure or a day of forgetting. This respite is as essential to the work of grief as the bad times. We need them if we are to go on and find a way of reconstructing our life without the person we have lost.

What if there are no 'good' or 'better' times? What if the sadness seems unrelenting and each moment of each day is equally devoid of meaning? What if there is no energy, what if sleep is seriously disturbed - and from the early hours of the morning to the last thing at night, everything is grey and purposeless?

Then it is possible that we may be suffering from depression, and it would be sensible to gather up what little energy we have left and go to see a doctor.

Factors Affecting Grief
"How long am I going to feel like this?"

It is impossible to predict the length of grief. We know that it does not last for ever, and we know that a major bereavement cannot be 'got over' or 'recovered from' in a matter of weeks or even months. The effects of the death of someone we love will be with us in one way or another for the rest of our life. This is not to say we will grieve for ever - because we won't.

It may seem impossible to believe in the early days of grief, but we will learn to laugh again and love again and we will not always feel as we do now.

How we will cope with our grief will depend partly on our own personal history. Our history will include our previous experiences of loss, and our experiences of love and security - for out of both of these have developed the inner strengths and personal resources we are able to draw upon at times of crisis and need.

The nature of the relationship between ourself and the person who has died will also help to determine the length and depth of the grief we experience. What has gone out of life because of that loss will influence our feelings and indicate just how much we will need to reconstruct our life after the death.

The circumstances leading up to and surrounding the death will have an influence on us and our feelings. How a death occurs is important. The impact of a sudden death will be different from the anticipated loss following a long illness.

The amount of support and help we have around us at the time of the death and in the months following it will also affect how we grieve.

HISTORY

LEARNING ABOUT LOSS

Bereavement is the loss through death of someone to whom we have a strong attachment. Our lives and theirs are joined together in one way or another. Death breaks that connection and we are bereaved.

How we will cope with such a loss will partially depend on our experiences of it in the past. We first learn about loss as a child. However secure parents try to make their children feel, and however much they may seek to protect them from the dangers of the outside world, they can never fully achieve this. The process of growing up involves both change and loss.

To Have And Have Not

Babies are very aware of their needs for comfort, nourishment and warmth. As tiny infants we all protested loudly if those needs were not met by the adults around us. We carry into adulthood this principle of 'have' and 'have not'.

As we grow-up, we develop expectations and assumptions that certain things will happen and certain people will be there. We have begun to attach ourselves to the world around us. If any of these attachments are broken we will react, even if our basic needs are not threatened. We have discovered loss.

Very young children are vulnerable at times of loss and change because they don't understand words. You can't explain to a baby that it is in hospital for its own good, or that it is only to be there for a day or a week. Babies and young children exist in a world where their needs are either met - or not met.

Learning About Loss

The small child experiments with loss. Games such a peek-a-boo and hide and seek condition a child to the idea that nothing ever stays quite the same. Children learn that things - and people - go away and come back again. The toddler in its pram will infuriate its mother by repeatedly throwing its toys out onto the ground, each time waiting for them to be picked up and returned. A special blanket or toy can become a transitional object; something that represents the mother or father and all the security they contain. As long as the child has this special object then he or she can allow the parent to go from their sight. In this way we are taught - and teach ourselves - about survival.

Temporary Loss

All small children parted from their source of 'mothering' will cry for its return. If this fails, they may become depressed. Eventually, the screams will turn into a more withdrawn kind of behaviour - sitting quietly in the cot - and this may be mistakenly interpreted as being 'good' or as 'settling down well'.

A little child needs mothering. If its own mother is not there, others can supply this, but it is not enough for a child simply to have its basic needs for survival met. He or she needs to be held and comforted.

Minor Loss

The growing child confronts loss time and again - a favourite toy disappears, a best friend moves away from the neighbourhood. There can even be a sense of loss when a special pair of trousers or jumper becomes too small and is thrown away or passed onto a younger brother or sister. That move from nursery school - away from where everything is familiar, to the strangeness of 'big school' - can be experienced as a most disturbing loss.

Some losses create fear or sadness, others just a passing moment of regret. It is through such losses we begin to perceive that nothing remains quite the same for ever. As long as the important things continue, as long as we remain part of a reasonably stable family-type group and are cared for and looked after, then the other losses quickly become accepted. Our new school becomes familiar, we make new best friends and play with as much pleasure with our new toys.

Discovering Death

Children are constantly discovering new words and each new word opens up a new way of thinking. It would be unusual for a child not to have discovered the word death or dead before the age of five. Television is full of death and so is the world around them - they will see dead birds, plants, insects; they may even have had a family pet that died and have held it in their hands, feeling how its cold hardness differed from the soft warmth of the living creature.

Death Is Forever

The idea that death is the final and permanent ending of life as we know it on this earth develops over the years. There is some dispute over the rate of this development; and children will naturally vary in this, as they do in other aspects of their growth.

A child, who is given clear, accurate information about death is obviously at an advantage. If the information has been unclear, hesitantly imparted and has changed from source to source, it may be little wonder that, when questioned about death, a child will simply reflect back that confusion.

It is possible that children are better able to understand and accept death than adults. After all, they are in the business of learning new concepts every day. Their minds are unclouded by what they should or ought to believe and better able to take in simple and straight-forward new information.

Bang Bang - You're Dead!

Young children play games based on killing - and being killed - as they experiment with new notions of power. To adults, this game-playing may seem proof that children don't understand death at all, the victim rising in time for tea or to take his or her turn as being the killer. Of course, this is to forget that children are actually very aware that a game has a different set of rules to those of life itself.

It is through such games that they are able to explore the complexity of the world about them and gradually learn how to deal with it.

The Learning Goes On

That process of learning about life and death goes on and on as the years pass. It does not stop when we are eight, 18, or 108. Each new situation involving loss will teach us something further about ourselves and this world that we live in.

OUR OWN STORY

Looking Back

How we deal personally with a bereavement will depend partly on our own personal history.

It can be helpful to look back over the events of our past and see how they may have influenced how we are thinking and feeling. Some people make a simple life chart, placing either side of a horizontal line all the large happenings in their life. The positive events go on one side of the line and the negative, bad things on the other side. The further from the line the more extreme the event. others prefer just to write down in date-order all the important good and bad things that have happened so far.

Whatever method chosen, it quickly gives us a picture of our past. We may have suffered other bereavements or have had to face other major losses, perhaps of a much-loved home, or a parent through separation, or a very close friend.

This, our latest, and perhaps greatest, loss becomes, itself, a part of the history of the life we are creating, simply and inescapably by living it.

Just as those other good and bad events affected us in the past, so this one will also affect us. Just as the line continued on past those other events, so the line of our life will also continue on past this major loss.

Making Comparisons

If we have suffered a previous loss through death and remember how we felt at the time, we will naturally make comparisons between our feelings then and those we are now experiencing.

We may find similarities or great differences between that past and this present.

In looking back at a past bereavement we may feel the sadness and pain all over again *plus* an additional sadness. Alongside our present grief we will also be carrying - for a while - those feelings from our past losses.

Failure To Grieve

Many people feel anxiety over the thought that, somehow, they failed to grieve properly for a past bereavement, remembering they didn't cry or that there was no-one to talk to at the time.

It is important to hold onto the fact that it is not essential to cry or talk or attend a funeral in order to grieve. Mostly, if our feelings are not given the opportunity of coming to the surface they will go underground and the work of grief will take place on a different level. One way or another we will have learnt to live on after that past bereavement because we are still here now - the proof of living is life.

The Value Of Going Back

If we sense the need to feel some of the emotions associated with a past loss it is not because we failed to grieve properly in the past, but because this present loss has given us a valuable opportunity to re-explore ourselves and our history. In the exploration of our past we will learn about ourselves, what we were and the person we have become.

Carrying Things Forward

It is not just one or two isolated major events that create the person we are, and in concentrating on those large happenings we may forget the less dramatic day-to-day accumulation of what we give, and what we get.

If we have been helped to grow up seeing ourselves as a reasonably OK person, capable of being loved and of loving, then, whatever battering our self-image may get at a time of bereavement, we will be able to hold onto that belief in ourselves.

If we have always been seen as a vulnerable person then we may feel overwhelmed by our loss. How can such a vulnerable person as ourselves be expected to cope with so much pain and disturbance?

The definitions we have inherited from our childhood carry on affecting us long after we have grown up and out-grown them. Major life-changing events can help us re-assess ourselves, and it is possible to discover that we possess strengths and vulnerabilities that we never knew existed before the crisis.

Religion

We carry many things with us out of our childhood which will affect how we grieve the death of someone we care for.

If we have strong religious beliefs, these will help us form a clear personal picture of death and what takes place after death. This can bring comfort at a time when it is most needed.

The belief that we will definitely join up with the one who has died after our own death can take away some of the pain of bereavement because it gives hope for the future.

Religious belief may give a sense of purpose and meaning to a death which, without it, might appear senseless. Even if the meaning behind the death is obscure it is possible to see it as part of a larger plan beyond our comprehension.

Sometimes our views may conflict with those of our friends or our family. Many people find that they question their beliefs after a major bereavement. How can we trust a God who is capable of snatching from us the very thing we value most? How could He allow the good to suffer and the bad to go unpunished?

Talking to a minister of religion can help us to work through the deep and complex questions that can arise after a major bereavement.

The Forever Loss

Few of us, whatever our age, reach the point when we can say that we have developed a total understanding of death. Concepts such as 'for ever', 'eternity', are difficult ones to grasp. It is hard to imagine the world going on without us - when the world as we know it is perceived through our eyes.

The Child In All Of Us

Whatever our age, we continue to be a child and to be childish. Usually this side of ourself is balanced and moderated by our more controlled 'adult' and 'parent' side.

After the loss of someone we love, the 'child' part of us may cry out for comfort and for attention. We may feel lost and alone - just like a small child.

Moving On

Ultimately the greatest honour we can do those we love who have died is to take the best of what they gave us and carry it forward into our future with respect and appreciation. If we are monitoring ourselves carefully then we will recognise when we reach the point where we need to give ourselves permission to move forward, away from the past and our grief; a time when it is right to take on new responsibilities, make new relationships and create the new future that belongs to us and us alone. To do so is not a denial of the importance of the person who died but rather a celebration of their life and of the rich inheritance of learning, thoughts and memories they gave us.

Death teaches us a great deal. Perhaps its greatest lesson is the fact that nothing lasts for ever. Not even sadness and grief. Experience of loss can make us aware of the preciousness of life and our need to make the very most of the time we have on this earth.

WHO DIED?

Each of us lives at the centre of our own personal network of relationships. At the heart of the system are those who are most important to us, perhaps our parents, other relatives, our wife or husband, our children, our lovers or our closest friends.

The grief we feel when we lose someone whom we love deeply can seem unbearable. It overwhelms every part of our life. Such intense feelings will be different to those experienced after the loss of a less important person in our life. We will still grieve. We will still be sad and distressed, but the meaning of our life will not be as seriously disturbed as after the death of a very close relative or friend.

Each person in our life will have a special part to play and, the importance of those parts will change as we change over the years. Because of this, it is not easy to predict how we will grieve a particular loss. We may find we are not reacting in the way that we would have expected, that we are overwhelmed by the loss of someone we have not seen for years, or hardly affected at all by the death of someone, without whom, at one time, we would have thought we could never live.

A Change Of Label

Some bereavements change the label society gives us; the death of both our parents will mean that we become an orphan. The death of a husband or wife makes us a widow or widower. The death of an only sibling (brother or sister) may mean that we will never be a brother or sister to anyone ever again. The death of our first or only child robs us of the title of parent.

Losing A Role In Life

When we are bereaved we lose not just that real, actual, living person who was a part of our life; we lose also the particular role we gained through the fact that their life and ours was joined together in that special way.

Each close relationship we make with another human being is unique. We may be seen by someone as having a sense of humour, or as being intelligent, or a great lover. When the relationship ends, then those special unique qualities in ourselves seem to disappear as well. Now there is no one to see how clever or funny we are, no one to be a great lover with. It is as if parts of ourself have been lost for ever.

The Temporary Loss Of What We Are
This is not a permanent loss - although it appears to be when we are in the early weeks and months of our bereavement. In time, we will be able to re-discover those qualities within ourselves; perhaps through other important relationships which will give us the opportunity to be funny and clever and in love once again. The good we have experienced is never lost. It remains in us, part of us until such time as it is able to be used once again.

Practical Changes
Some bereavements will create the need for great changes in the day-to-day running of our life. The death of a parent may mean we have to leave our family home and move into a flat, or, alternately it might mean we have to think seriously about giving up our hard won independence to take care of a remaining parent or a younger brother or sister.

Plans for the future may have to be shelved because of the death. It may be necessary financially to give up college and go out to work, or to give up a present job in order to take over responsibility for a family business.

Such major life-changes will affect how we grieve. The loss extends beyond the person who is dead and into the structure of our present life. When we long for the deceased person to come back we may also be longing for a return to that better past which once contained so much hope and promise.

Inheritance
All of us will leave something behind us when we die. Our ideas and actions and thoughts will live on in the memories of those closest to us. What possessions or money we have will pass onto those who follow after us.

Objects that pass from generation to generation within a family assume importance because they carry with them history and a sense of belonging.

If we are relatively young it is more likely we will inherit the family nose rather than the family silver. Genetic inheritance contains its own value; it too enables us to see ourselves as part of a larger unit. We have not sprung from nowhere, we are a part of a family, and we have a sense of our ancestry.

Objects act as a link between us and the one we have lost. It can help to actually hold something that belonged to the dead person, it does not have to be valuable, just something that reminds us particularly of them - a pen or a piece of clothing.

Photographs can be copied and enlarged and they can act as a very valuable reminder of the one we have lost. The pain and sadness we may feel when we first look at them can be gradually transformed into pleasure as we think back over the good times of the past.

Loss Of The Future And Loss Of The Past

The death of a member of our childhood family can seem as if we have lost the past itself. A dear grandparent can take with them our childhood; when they are no longer there we are no longer a grandchild. We grow up quite suddenly with their death.

The death of a baby or a child robs us of our future. All the hopes and plans we built into our life through them are stolen away.

Secret Losses

Sometimes the world recognises no connection between us and the one we are grieving for. Perhaps the relationship we shared was a secret or perhaps it was simply not recognised for what it was. Its importance was underrated. Possibly, even we did not see just how lost we would feel without it.

It is hard to grieve alone, to have no acknowledgement of our sadness and pain.

One Death: Many Bereavements

Each death will have its own special significance for those who are bereaved by it.

One man's death might mean the loss of a husband to a wife, the loss of a father to his children and the loss of a son to his parents. Through that same man's death a brother may be lost, and a cousin or a nephew. A work mate may lose a colleague, a neighbour disappears, a darts team finds itself without a valuable member and several people lose a good and trusted friend.

Each of the people who knew the deceased will be grieving for the special loss that they have suffered. A surprisingly high number of lives can be affected by one single death.

Some grief reactions - shock, the need to know how and why it happened, a feeling of sadness and personal vulnerability in the face of death - may be experienced by all who knew the man or woman who has died but the impact of the loss will vary greatly from person to person.

The darts team will be able to find another member for its games. The job will be advertised and eventually another work colleague will sit at the empty desk. It is not possible so easily to replace the position of a father, or mother or a brother or daughter.

Close friends may grieve deeply, but the death will not affect them in the same way as a wife or husband who may have lost a financial supporter as well as a lover and a best friend.

After a major bereavement the impact of the loss suffered will be related to the meaning and importance of the relationship that existed between the deceased and the bereaved.

There will be differences in our reactions to the loss of a parent and the loss of a sister; between the loss of a little baby and the loss of a close friend.   Each loss we experience has its own unique significance for us.

A DEATH IN THE FAMILY

The majority of us spend our early years as part of a family group. For better or worse, that group provides us with all the essentials for growth and survival; food, a roof over our head, warmth, clothing, companionship and the opportunity to learn from those around us.

A family group can be small and insular, giving few opportunities to learn from sources outside the home. Or, it may be a flexible and extended unit containing regular contact with many other adults and children; perhaps step-brothers and sisters, grandparents, aunts and uncles, child minders, close family friends and neighbours.

Whatever the size of the group the loss of a family member will have far-reaching implications for everyone within it.

Who's Who?
Except at Christmas, few of us take the time and trouble to note down all the 'important' people in our life. We are so used to them being there that we tend to assume their presence or forget them altogether. This is particularly true when we are low and it appears that no one cares for us, or when we are concentrating hard on a personal event; an exam, a new love affair or problem at work. At such times our families exist only as a background to what we see as the real business of living.

The death or serious illness of someone in our family may force us to re-evaluate our priorities, and we may suddenly find ourselves focusing on the world around us in a very different way.

Growing Up
For years our family home may have been our only safe place; the focus of all our dreams and fears and needs. In our late teens or early twenties it gradually becomes the place we live in until such time as we are ready to move on. As we reach a point where college, jobs and new relationships begin to take us regularly away from home it rapidly ceases to be the centre of our existence.

The older we are, the greater our wish for independence. The practice of distancing ourselves from the immediate family is essential if we are eventually to live apart from our parents and establish a base of our own.

Moving On
Generally this process of moving on takes place in that decade which lies somewhere between our late teens and the end of our twenties. The urge towards independence starts much earlier, perhaps as soon as we reach puberty and begin to think of ourselves as sexual beings. There is evidence that young people are delaying their ultimate exit from the family home later and later, perhaps due to the increased cost of setting up home. It is impossible to move on until we have somewhere to go and the financial means to support ourselves. Families can come under strain when older adult children are obviously ready to move on but are unable to do so because of the high cost of housing or difficulty of getting a job.

Family Conflict
Although some adolescents find the years between 13 and 20 relatively peaceful, many do not. It is not unusual for conflicts between teenager and parents to arise and there can be a fair amount of sibling rivalry also, at this stage, as brothers and sisters vie for best position in the family and compete with one another for attention and love.

Everyone A Loser
A death in a family will affect all members of that group. When a group of people are bereaved, they have to find a way of sharing the loss. Whilst each member will struggle to cope with their own personal loss, they will also have to deal with the loss suffered by the other members of the group.

Very often the group acknowledges the grief of one member as being more overwhelming than that of another. It is not unusual for one family member to carry the grief for a while, perhaps because they were particularly close to the person who has died or because they are seen as the most vulnerable one. In time, this person may get better and another take on the role of main griever. There is no way we can exist in a vacuum when living in a family group, however isolated and different from the others we may be feeling. How we will grieve will be affected by our relatives' grief, just as their feelings will be moderated by our own.

THE DEATH OF A GRANDPARENT

It is possible that, by the time we reach our late teens and twenties, we will already have lost at least one of our grandparents. We may only have very hazy pictures of those long-ago characters from our early childhood, and very little memory, if any at all, of how they died or their funeral services.

In later years, as an older child or a young adult, the death of our grandfather or grandmother is likely to be our first major bereavement and our first personal confrontation with death. As such it will have a deep significance above and beyond our individual sense of loss and sadness.

Personal Loss

The relationship between grandparent and grandchild can be a very special one. Grandparents can and often do, play a unique part in their grandchildren's lives. Some live close enough to act as substitute mums and dads. They baby-sit, pick their grandchildren up from school, have them for holidays or when they are sick. They are there at times of trouble and at times of happiness and have been a part of their grandchildren's lives for as long as they can remember. To lose such a grandparent is to lose so much, for when they die all the security and love and care they have contributed for so long seems to die with them. For a while the world can appear a rather lonely and insecure place in which to live.

Grandads and grandmas that live further away can still play an important part in their grandchild's life. Visits can be looked forward to with pleasure and letters and telephone calls can bridge the gaps between meetings.

Grandparents have been described as having all the fun of parenthood with non of the responsibility - and grandparents are often in a unique position to enjoy their grandchildren. Retired people may have time to talk or listen or tell stories or play games; the kind of spare time which busy working parents simply do not have.

Some grandparents are more distant figures. They are the provider of gifts at Christmas and at birthdays. Rare family visits may be times when everyone is on their very best behaviour with all the tension that this creates. However, even a remote grandmother or grandfather can play an important part in their grandchild's life. They may have a real influence on how the children in the family are educated or brought up. As long as they are alive certain family rules are obeyed. They have a position of authority over their children and what they think, say and do has an effect. This may only become apparent when they are no longer there.

If our parents have been in conflict with their parents (which might account for the lack of regular contact and the tension) then a death can shift and disturb those complex patterns that underlie family relationships.

Our Parents Lose A Parent

At the same time that we lose a grandparent, one of our parents will lose a parent. The loss of a parent is a major bereavement whatever our age.

How our parent will cope with that loss will depend on the closeness of the relationship they shared with their parent and what it was that went from their life when the death happened. They may have lost their best friend, their own source of support and security. If the relationship was a difficult one, complicated by quarrels and anger, they may have lost forever the chance to put things right.

Alongside their own sadness, our mother or father may also have to support a deeply grieving, remaining parent. Perhaps their own feelings may have to be pushed into the background as they care for those around them.

We watch our parents go about the practical and emotional business of death and, perhaps for the first time, we recognise that a time will come when we will be in their position and it will become our responsibility to arrange for their burial or cremation.

It is possible that our parents may also be thinking of their own future death. The death of their parent may have exposed them to an awareness of their own mortality. Such thoughts are not morbid. They are a natural and a sensible way for us to prepare ourselves for what lies ahead.

Grandparents Come In Pairs

Of course not all grandparents come in pairs; if the partner of the grandparent we have just lost is already dead or lost long ago from our lives through separation or divorce, then there will be no surviving grandmother or grandfather. But if this death breaks up a loving couple then, as a grandchild, we may find that, not only have we lost one grandparent but our relationship with our remaining grandparent has also been considerably changed.

Our remaining grandparent may be grieving at such a deep level that they have no time now for us and our needs. All the comfort and pleasure of the past can seem to disappear in the early months of grief and it may be some time before our grandparent is able to reach across that gulf of despair and include us and others into their life once more.

Alternately, and this does occasionally happen, a grandparent may feel that the only reason they have to live on, lies in their love for a particular grandchild. That child or young person may find themselves having to take on a new role in the family - one that carries a very heavy responsibility. However much we may care for a grandparent we cannot become their sole support or reason for existence. Perhaps the greatest help we can give lies in letting our grandfather or grandmother know that they still have an important role to play in our lives.

Our First Funeral

Marriages, christenings and funerals are the large occasions that bring a family together and our grandparent's funeral will be a family affair. We watch as our parents, uncles and aunts, nieces and nephews, in-laws and all those other relatives who may not have seen one another for years, join together publicly in acknowledging the importance of the death. This day will be a landmark in the history of the family. Each person's private personal grief is absorbed into the larger public sense of loss.

Although we may be expected to attend the funeral and take part in the gathering afterwards, if our grandparent's partner or our parents are still alive, we will not be responsible for its organisation. This will give us a valuable opportunity both to learn about the practicality involved in such an event and also it may allow us to face the emotional impacts of death and bereavement from a relatively secure position.

Apart from the fact that we have lost someone we cared for and who cared for us, the realisation that the coffin we can see and actually touch contains the body of someone so recently alive can be a moving and disturbing experience. The laying of that body into the earth, or the closing of the curtains behind it in the crematorium, all these are highly emotive happenings.

The Death Of An Era

The death of a grandparent or a great-grandparent can mark the end of an era. The senior members of a family may play an important part in the structure of the family group and when they die it is altered. Perhaps a particular elderly person acted as the focal point for all the generations and for the different sides of the family. When they die a hole appears in the centre of the group, perhaps one from which it never quite recovers.

Our grandparent may be the last person in our family to treat us as a child and when they die it can seem like the death of childhood itself. Sometimes we lose our grandparent at the very time when we are in the process of moving away from our childhood and becoming an adult. Then the two separate losses appear to combine into one large ending.

Becoming A Part Of History

The history of a family is passed on from one generation to the next and our grandparents are an important link in that continuing chain. Their experiences are passed through us, onto our children, who will, in turn, pass stories of the long-distant past down to their own children and grandchildren.

If we have had a good relationship with a grandparent there will be sadness when they die but their death cannot take that precious past away from us. Those good memories are our inheritance and we will carry them with us into our future.

THE DEATH OF UNCLES AND AUNTS

The wider family which lies outside our immediate home can play an important part in our growing up; inspite of the fact that we may only see these more distant relatives once or twice a year.

Some aunts and uncles will pass from our lives with very little effect; their death causing only a day or so of sadness; a short period when we relive memories from our childhood before moving back once again into the here-and-now of busy daily life.

Someone Special

The death of other relatives may create a special sense of loss because that particular person played a special part in our life.

Contact often becomes increasingly irregular as the years pass and the demands of our new life as young adults takes us out of the family circle. The knowledge that Aunty always says she adores our Christmas present, or that Uncle is always pleased if we happen to remember his birthday remains with us, but it may not be until someone dies that we realise a source of affection and real love, albeit distant, has passed from our life for ever. Then, perhaps at the moment of its passing, we become aware for the first time just how precious that particular relationship was, and how much we are going to miss it.

Saying Goodbye

If the seriousness of an illness is acknowledged openly, there may be an opportunity to visit the dying person and tell them how much we have valued their love and care over the years. But often there is no time for such proper endings, and we are left with all the unsaid thank-yous and acknowledgements running around in our head.

It is always sad when there is no chance to say goodbye, but relationships which have lasted a lifetime often have no need for words.

Family Roots

When we are in the middle of that long process of moving away from our family and forging an independent life of our own; where we have come from may seem to be of little importance. At a time when we may be doing our best to escape the restrictions placed on us by our parents, our feelings of family loyalty are probably at an all-time low.

In spite of this, our uncles and our aunts, our grandparents and our cousins are woven through the history of our growing up. None of them may be vital to our daily existence and yet, because of the part they have played and will continue to play in who we are and what we are, they are all of some importance to us.

When we meet them at family weddings, christenings and funerals, they see in us both the person we are now and the person we used to be. They can see the changes in us and we can see the changes that time has made on them.

As long as they remain alive we have a yardstick by which we can measure our progress.

Permanent Standards

We can go on measuring ourselves against such family standards even if the people who created those standards have died. We know if so-and-so would have approved of a certain action or not. We remember what they found funny and what they disliked. We may find echoes of those standards in how we deal with our own children.

It is not important whether we liked or did not like a certain relative. We can value them for their strength or their pigheadedness or some other aspect of their character. The fact that they existed makes our personal story that much richer.

At some point in our life we will find ourselves saying, "I had an Aunt once who ..." or, "My uncle used to ..."

THE DEATH OF A PARENT

The death of a parent is a major bereavement. As a young child our very survival is dependent on adults - and usually our parents. They provide us with shelter, food and warmth. Apart from these basic needs, our parents or substitute parents fulfil many other important functions.

The loss of a parent is made up of a multitude of other losses. We will grieve not just for the man or woman who was our dad or mum but also for the loss of everything they provided as our father or mother.

Parents are useful. By understanding their importance we are better able to understand our own loss when they die.

Long Term Security/Staying Alive

A child psychiatrist once said that parents have only one real obligation to their children, and that is to remain alive. Sadly no parent can guarantee that they will definitely live until the point when their children no longer need them. Over 180,000 children in Britain under the age of 16 have lost a parent through death. Children do not automatically cease to be a child or stop needing their parents just because they have reached the age of 16.

The relationship between a child and its parent is a deep and a complex one which does not lose its significance simply because a child moves away from home or becomes an adult in his or her own right.

The Family Structure

The majority of children in this country still grow up in a two-parent family which has at its head a mother and a father. By watching their parents, children learn that women behave in such a way and men in another. This information is then contrasted with other adult behaviour outside the family.

Through their parents, children receive first-hand experience of mothering and fathering, and this, in turn, becomes the basis on which they will build their own family structures at a later date.

If a parent dies, an opportunity to learn about male and female roles is lost. The structure of a family is seriously disrupted by the death of a mother or father.

Parents As Homemakers

Most parents devise a system for sharing the work-load involved in running a home. When a parent dies this means that everyone left behind in the family will have to take on a greater burden if the home is to continue to run smoothly. Where a family has contained a very sick parent for a long time, the normal household routines may already have had to be altered. The sudden ending of the life of a parent means these changes will have to happen almost overnight. All too easily the house can seem to fall apart. Things slip rapidly out of control and the task of bringing them back into order can seem a daunting one. Alongside the shock and exhaustion of grief, death brings its own heavy work-load of probate and business matters which need to be completed in the early months following the loss. It may be some time before new routines are developed.

Many people describe how they feel the heart of the home has seemed to disappear when a father or a mother dies. What once seemed to contain love and order and security can appear to be only a place of survival, especially in the early days of loss when everything is at its blackest.

Parents As Rule-Makers

Part of the work of being a parent is the need to teach children a code of behaviour that will enable them to operate successfully in the world outside the home. This is partly done by setting an example which the child can copy, and partly by laying down a set of rules defining what is OK and what is not.

This set of rules is constantly changing. It is not alright for a child of two to cross the road on their own, but perfectly alright when they are ten.

As the child grows older, what is expected of him or her changes. In an ideal world this process goes smoothly. Few of us, however, live in an ideal world - nor do we grow up in a world inhabited solely by our parents. We will also have our friends, who will have their own set of rules and standards - perhaps very different from those of our parents.

As children, we have developed through a process of confrontation, challenge and acceptance. This process is disturbed by the death of a parent. The remaining parent may find it hard to re-enforce rules when they are vulnerable and sad. Alternately they may be over-strict in a desperate attempt to keep things in order.

It can be hard to lose a parent when one is right in the middle of a period of confrontation or challenge. It is as if life freezes over and we are left to mentally replay the same scenes of anger again and again. Given time, our feelings and those of the other person would, quite naturally, have developed and changed. Sadly, death has ended that process of natural development.

Family Battles

We learn an enormous amount about relationships and human behaviour from our parents and close relatives. We learn that it is possible to be angry and disappointed and let down and still remain together in a useful partnership. The family, at its best, is a safe place where the necessary battles that lead to development take place. We are not sacked the first time we break the rules - as we might be from a job.

Death may seem to destroy this safe place. The extreme emotions generated in a family in the months following the bereavement can seriously disrupt its sense of stability. The pain of loss can generate intense reactions, sudden quarrels may break out, quarrels which do not fade away after a good night's sleep.

When one is grieving deeply, one's vision of the world around can be distorted. Little remarks which would have been shrugged off before the death assume enormous importance. Everything can seem unbearable and incapable of ever getting any better, especially in those terrible early months of bereavement. At such a time it is important to recognise the cause of some of these quarrels - they happen because everyone is hurting inside. If we can understand the anger it becomes just a little easier to bear.

As we lose a parent, so our parent loses a partner. How they deal with their loss will affect our ability to deal with the personal loss that we have suffered.

The End Of That 'Perfect 'Partnership

The ending of the 'perfect' marriage through death will leave the remaining partner overwhelmed by their sadness and loss. At such a time they may feel that there is no point in life anymore without the one they loved. Everything around them fades into insignificance when compared to the loss they have suffered.

Having lost one parent, children are faced with the prospect of losing the other who may be openly expressing the wish to die. Lost in their own private world of grief and overcome by pain and sadness, they may have become incapable of connecting up with those around them - even their own children.

Sometimes a newly bereaved parent will cling to their older children, desperately needing them near, relying on them for comfort and practical advice.

Many older children find that their own feelings of grief and sadness have to be put to one side as they take on the job of supporting their parent. When faced with so much distress it can be hard to hold on to the fact that a parent is a parent and a child remains a child whatever the circumstances and whatever the ages of parent and child.

As a child we can offer our parents our skills and our love but we cannot and should not become their parent and attempt to control their lives or take responsibility for them. Sometimes we can help them most by letting them know that we need them to go on being our parent and caring for us.

Temporary Troubles

Not all husbands and wives spend all of their married lives agreeing with one another or living in perfect harmony and bliss. Most marriages go through periods of strain and disagreement. Even if our parents are going through a particularly difficult time, they may still have no intention of ending the marriage in divorce. It is especially sad when a fundamentally good marriage is suddenly ended in death at such a time. The problems and anger that seemed so all-consuming a short time ago fall into perspective and appear meaningless compared to the life that has been shared together and all the future years which have been lost forever.

If a couple have been shouting at each other only a moment before, how can the one left behind suddenly be weeping and expressing undying love for their dead partner the next? Such behaviour can seem hypocritical to family members who know the tensions and rows that have been taking place. But it isn't.

Death robs us of the chance to make things better; to say, "I'm sorry, it was only a passing stage, it wasn't really important."

When we grieve we grieve for the loss of the whole relationship, not just for the last few weeks or years of it. A wife may mourn the loss of the young man she married. She may mourn the loss of the father of her children, the man she loved once so much and the man that she might possibly have loved again.

Parents At War

Sometimes the problems parents face become too great and the marriage breaks down ending in separation or divorce. The children in such a family may lose contact with one or other of their parents because of emotional pressure or because one moves far away. An absent or bad parent can be the focus of a great deal of anger. If such a parent dies it can be hard to know what to do with all that left-over anger. And of course, as long as the absent parent was alive somewhere there was always the chance that, at some point in the future, things could have been put right. Death ends such hopes.

If children do manage to maintain links with both their parents, the death of one of these warring parents can make it exceptionally hard for a young person to find the space to grieve. Their remaining parent may be dealing with complex reactions of anger, recrimination, guilt and perhaps even relief that a painful situation is now over. The child or children may feel very alone in their grief, and their version of the past and what has been lost will be very different from that of their parent.

The Split Family

Today many young people grow up in families where their mother and their father are either technically separated, divorced, or, for one reason or another, living in separate homes. One, or both parents may have remarried.

Even when a divorce has divided a couple many years ago there can still be grief when an ex-partner dies; sadness for lost opportunities and a fresh realisation of the real goodness and worth of that person.

If we are a single parent bringing up our children on our own then we may have relied very heavily on our mother or father to help us care for our children. When they die it is as if we have lost a partner in life.

Family Favourites

Although few parents admit to having favourites we all know that each child has its own special position in the family. We may be seen as taking after our dad, or being just like our mum! Whether this is a compliment or a criticism will depend on the circumstances surrounding the remark. And, as children, we will have favourites between our mother and our father. Usually this is part of the natural process of development. We may start off wanting and needing our mother - who is generally the provider of our early care. This may be followed by a change of allegiance - as we transfer affections to our father.

Many teenagers come into direct conflict with one or other of their parents. It is not at all unnatural to feel that one hates one's mother or father. Given time these intense feelings will give way to less extreme ones. There probably isn't a teenager in this country who hasn't secretly wished one or other of their parents dead at some point in their life.

Where death steps in and takes away the parent we are angry with, we do not have the opportunity to grow through such a stage. We remain at that point of anger; confused, deeply unhappy and perhaps secretly wondering if our hatred was a cause of their death.

Alternately, if the 'good' parent dies leaving us alone with the one we were most angry with, then it is possible that our anger will increase. We may even find ourselves blaming them for failing to care for the parent we have lost.

Being angry with one's parents is a perfectly natural part of the developmental process from childhood to independent adult. There will be many times when parents will be justifiably angry with their children. We cannot expect our parents to be perfect; they simply have to be 'good enough' parents to ensure that we grow up reasonably healthy in mind and body.

Bad Parents

Some parents are not good enough parents. This may be because they had bad parenting when they were a child. But, for whatever reason, they have gone on to make serious mistakes in parenting their own child or children.

Perhaps they have been unable to control their sexual feelings, and these have spilled over into their relationships with their children. Perhaps they have been unable to control their anger and rage. What should have been proper discipline has changed into harsh and inappropriate punishment.

Perhaps they have been unable to deal with their relationship with their partner, and this has caused real pain and disruption in the family.

It may seem to be a much easier job to deal with the death of a bad parent. Why shouldn't we be relieved that, at long last, all the anxiety and pain they brought into our lives has gone for ever? And why shouldn't we be pleased at the prospect of being free to live our life as we want to?

Strangely, however, alongside these feelings of relief and release we may find ourselves crying out for our dead parent, and discover deep inside, an unexpected pool of pain and sadness. Other people, knowing our previous feelings for our parent, will find it hard to understand why we should seem to be grieving for such a person. We too, may be surprised at these unlikely reactions.

Why should we grieve for someone who has brought us pain and unhappiness? Because they were our parent, and their death - for better or worse - does matter to us. We may grieve because they were not always a bad parent, and we can cry out for the better times that we had before the bad times began.

It is possible to grieve for the loss of the good parent we never had, and for what we can never have now. Death has prevented any hope that things could get better in the future. All chance of reconciliation or revenge is gone for ever.

Following In The Shoes Of A 'Perfect' Parent
It is not easy to be the son or daughter of a dead parent who is seen as being 'perfect'. How can we ever hope to follow in their footsteps? How great our mistakes seem against their perfection.

When we lose someone we love, we tend to see only the goodness they brought to life, especially in the early months of bereavement. The loss of their love and presence is so great it is almost impossible to concentrate on their ordinary, normal failings, which anyway seem diminished by comparison with their good qualities.

We may see our dead parent as ideal; everything we would wish to be in the future. Such feelings help us to work harder to become like them, to achieve the goals they set for us, to be the kind of person they wanted us to be. In time a more rounded and more accessible portrait often emerges.

Substitute Mums And Dads
Not all children are brought up by their genetic mother and father. Sometimes other adults take over the job of caring for a child, perhaps grandparents or aunts and uncles, stepmums and dads, foster or adoptive parents. If someone was 'like a mother' or 'like a father' to us then we will grieve for them as if they were our mother or our father. Their death will leave us saddened and our world will be diminished because they are no longer a part of it.

Guarding Us From Death
Good or bad, our parents play vitally important parts in our lives. The parent of our own sex seems to stand like a guardian between us and our own ultimate death. As long as they are there, still living, we need not worry, but when they die we are exposed to the prospect of our own mortality. We become the next in line.

Going Ahead
There can also be great comfort in the knowledge that, whatever might lie beyond the grave, it has been made less fearful by the fact that a beloved parent has already gone ahead, and the way is made just that much safer for us through their death.

THE DEATH OF A FATHER

In the course of one day, many men in this country will die.

My Father

The death of this man is different. It is unique because we know this man, this man belonged to us. This man was our father and the relationship between him and us can never be repeated. No-one else can ever be our father or take his place in our life and, as his child, we will have had a unique place in his life and seen a side of him which will not have been apparent to his friends or work colleagues.

The Special Loss

We will also be aware that he felt differently towards us, than to any brothers or sisters we may have. Although the same man, the father that they have lost is not exactly the same as the father we have lost.

One way or another, he has been a part of our existence since our birth. If it was not for him we would not be here now. The us that is *us* has developed through him. Genetically and behaviourally he has influenced us and that influence will continue long after his death.

The Unique Man

This man who was our father will have had a particular personality. He will have smiled in a certain way, been angry about certain things, believed or not believed in God and the afterlife. He may have been an easy man to live with, or a challenging and difficult man. He will have had his good points and his bad points, his strengths and his weaknesses.

As his child there will have been times when we loved him, times when we found him impossible, times when he made us laugh and times when he made us cry.

He Was My Father

In the first days of bereavement the centre of attention very often falls on the widow and the huge loss that she has suffered and it can be easy to overlook an older child's sadness at the death of his or her father.

People rarely send condolence cards to younger people or write them letters acknowledging their special loss.

Adult children may be expected to share in the organisation of the funeral and be seen to be supportive to their mother. Their own feelings of confusion and numbness may have to be put to one side as they cope with new problems demanding new solutions.

Sometimes we have to find a private space at this difficult and demanding period and concentrate on the fact that this is our father that had died and that we too have a right to explore the personal loss that we have suffered.

Having One's Own Life

The fact that we may have a job, a girl- or boyfriend, a husband, even young children to care for, does not mean that we will necessarily be less affected by the death of our father. The fact that we love other people does not mean we will not grieve for the loss of the man who was so important to us.

The Role Of A Father

Each society has certain expectations of the roles we take on in our life.

We form a mental score-sheet of what a father is and the tasks he is expected to take on in the family. Very often that picture is a long way from reality, but even so, most of us judge our particular father against that score sheet, ticking off the ways he has succeeded and failed in meeting its expectations. When we lose a father, we lose not just the particular man that was our father, we also lose all the expectations and implications that having a father means.

The Loss Of Security

Many people equate having a man about the house with a sense of security. For all members of a family, the father can stand for safety - as long as he is there things will be alright. Even an ill father can hold a family together and provide it with a secure base.

If our father dies this sense of inner security can be disturbed. This can happen even if it is many years since we actually lived with our father or he had any real influence over our daily life. It is not uncommon for older, adult children who lose their father to feel deeply insecure for a while.

It is possible to develop fears and phobias in the weeks following the death and dealing with these can be intensely distressing. The death of a father may unleash very deep-seated feelings indeed.

Supplying The Money

It is a common assumption that a father will contribute towards the financial security of his family; that he will have a job and that his earnings will go towards supporting his wife and children.

In the imagined 'good old days' it was supposedly simple; men worked at their jobs and women worked in the home, caring for it and raising the children. Although this pattern still exists it is no longer quite so clear cut. In parts of the country, men might find it harder to get employment than their wives. The family income may be made up of state benefit and a wife's part-time earnings.

Fathers may be ill and unable to work, or, in some families, the roles are reversed by choice; the wife preferring to remain in her job and the father preferring to remain at home caring for the children. In many families both mother and father go out to work, although generally men earn more than women and contribute a higher amount to the family budget.

Where divorce or separation splits up parents, the budgeting can become confused, specially if step-fathers and mothers enter the family group.

Although financial support is seen as part of the tasks that a father takes on, the fact that a father may not support his children in this way does not mean that he cannot be a good and satisfactory father.

In reality many families are considerably worse off when a father dies, and this can add to the stress and difficulties experienced by all the family in the months following his death.

If we are in a position of benefiting financially through our father's death, we may find our feelings swinging between real satisfaction and a sense of guilt that our gain was acquired through his loss. It may be some time before we are able to see the gain for what it is, just one part of that much larger inheritance that all parents bequeath their children; that package deal containing life, genes, inherited characteristics, memories, emotional and financial support over many years and sometimes, after death - property, the family valuables or a sum of money. Perhaps the greatest sadness is the fact that they are not able to hear our thank-you.

Growing Up With A Man In The Home

The death of a father can deprive children of the experience of seeing, at close quarters, how a man lives. If there is no man in the family, even something so little as the fact that men shave every morning is simply not available to a young child.

It is possible to see what other's fathers do *outside* the home; they may pick up their children from school, or take them to football matches, or be there at open-evening, but it is much harder to see the contribution they make once they are inside the privacy of the home.

The Man Of The Family

As long as a family has a father, then there is no need for his role to be taken on by other family members. If a family becomes fatherless, then a mother or another relative may appoint one of the children as a kind of father figure. Sometimes, the eldest boy is told he is now 'man of the household' after his father's death. Girls too, can be expected to take on the tasks previously done by their father and it can be flattering to be seen as competent and adult.

Often the death of one of our parents forces us to grow up faster and to take on more responsibility within our family, but, a child cannot and should not be expected to take over an adult role.

Father The Rule-Maker

Very often the father is expected to be the disciplinarian of the family. It is he who must set the rules and apply punishment when necessary. Fortunately this pattern is changing, and it is rare now for children to be lined up in front of their father the moment he returns from work - their misdeeds related by their mother and the punishment rapidly administered. This system placed an enormous strain on all concerned and it is a miracle that any good father/child relationships managed to survive it.

Often our picture of our father is distorted by the fact that he has been the disciplinarian of the family. We may feel only able to remember the word 'no' or the anger when we broke the rules, and that burning sense of unfairness that all children feel from time to time. It is impossible to look ahead and be able to see that, in time, when that task of rule-making had been completed, then it would have been easier for a more equal relationship to develop between father and child.

Soft Father/Strict Mother

In some families, it is mother who makes the rules and applies the punishment when these are broken. Because father has, perhaps, been absent for some time and the hard work has fallen to her by default, or, it could be that the father is by nature a man who is hesitant to take on that role, and therefore it has been left to the mother to ensure that various standards of behaviour are upheld. This system creates the potential for imbalance and stress within a family. It is all too easy for children to see their father as a good and gentle person and mother as some kind of monster. If the father dies it can be difficult to complete the process where gradually we reach an understanding of the differing strengths and weaknesses of both parents. We are left with that good/bad picture in our mind.

The Loss Of A Partner

The wife of the man who has died is usually seen to be the main griever - the person who has lost the most and has the right to lead the mourning. She will be facing the loss of the man with whom she chose to share her life; who was probably also her lover, her closest friend and dearest companion.

It is impossible to take in the full impact of such a loss in a short space of time. Ahead of her lies the painful task of grieving, but, right from the first days of loss, she is aware that the structure of the family has been changed for ever. Where once there was a man, there is now only an empty space. A whole range of tasks and jobs go undone because the person who did those jobs is now dead.

Tasks will have to be re-distributed and everyone in a bereaved family may find that they have to carry a slightly heavier work-load after the death. Even younger children can be encouraged to contribute to the running of the household, perhaps by tidying away their toys or by making their beds in the morning.

It is intensely hard for a woman - who has been at the very heart of a demanding family - to find herself suddenly alone. It is hard to have to learn to live alone, sleep alone, eat alone, to have no-one there to talk things over with at the end of the day.

A mother grieving deeply for her dead husband may therefore find it almost impossible to reach out towards her children, and, for a while, children can suffer a double loss. Not only have they lost their father through death, but their mother is also lost to them because she is unable to comfort or support them at a time when they most need her. Sometimes another member of the family or a close family friend can help out until the mother begins to feel a little stronger.

Collapse Of A Mother

Some widows find that life in the early weeks following the death of their husband is almost unbearable. This is especially true if the death came suddenly, if the relationship between husband and wife was very close, or if the wife was particularly dependent - practically and emotionally - on her husband.

Having just lost their father, adult children may feel they are in danger of losing their mother as they watch her struggling to find a way of living on after the death of her husband. Most widows and widowers feel that life has precious little meaning or purpose to it in the early months after a loss. Generally, this feeling does not mean that the person is seriously contemplating ending their life. But, if there is any doubt about this then it is obviously sensible to err on the side of caution and inform the family doctor immediately; the responsibility for life rests with them.

Dependent Mothers

A mother who has been extremely dependent on her husband may transfer that dependence onto her son or daughter. It is as if they and they alone are capable of providing the security, advice, companionship and love so desperately needed.

At such a time it is important to hold on to the fact that no-one can take the place of the person who has died. All children can do is to provide as much support as possible at this painful time.

There are limits to how much time and commitment a grown-up child is able to give to a grieving parent. Recognising this fact enables partial but good help to be there for a long time. Because grief is long term this is vital - so much better than trying to do everything and failing.

The Usefulness Of Fathers

Fathers have many uses. They are often the car driver, the picker-up, and dropper-off at parties, school, and work. They can sometimes be relied upon for the odd five pounds when money gets short.

They may have contacts outside the home - at the pub, or club, or their work, which offer a valuable extension to one's own life.

Fathers can be great tellers of jokes. Fathers can put things in perspective when things get out of proportion. Many fathers can provide a hundred and one small services about the home which go virtually un-noticed until there is no-one there to do those particular jobs.

The Future Ahead

It may be that life seems to go on quite smoothly without father there, until we reach a turning point in our life, a twenty-first birthday, a marriage, or the birth of a child. It could be a period of trouble, a particular success, or even Father's Day, when suddenly we find ourselves longing for someone strong behind us, for our father.

A DAUGHTER LOSES A FATHER

The relationship between a daughter and her father changes over the years. There are times when daughters adore their dads and times when they find them a pain in the neck.

How their different characters mix together - the daughter's position in the family, and the particular stage in life which daughter and father are going through - will all play an important part in their feelings for one another at any one time.

My Princess

To some fathers, their daughter is their little princess. She is everything that is most perfect in womanhood. Periods of great closeness can develop between a daughter and a father. Similarities of interest, or, alternatively, the acknowledgement of real differences can bring the young female and the older man together in what is an almost perfect union. To lose such a relationship through death is to lose so much.

Growing Apart

However, some fathers find their daughter's developing sexuality and independence very hard to accept. They may feel that it is their place to defend their daughter's honour and virginity at all cost, and this will put them on a collision course. The average daughter fights hard for her right to have boyfriends and to enjoy the same privileges and freedom as her friends.

The Middle Path

Most father-daughter relationships manage to steer a middle path somewhere between those two extremes. But many daughters feel that, when their father dies, they lose the one man that found them perfect, and who was their defender and protector - even if it had been a long time since their father last saw them as his little princess or rushed to their defence.

Helping One Another

Many mothers and daughters are able to grieve together for the man they have lost, and the sharing of their sadness eventually helps both of them to begin to find a way of moving forward, away from the past and towards the creation of a new future. In spite of her own pain, the mother is able to reach out and comfort her daughter in her special loss and the daughter is able to see that her mother has her own private and personal areas of loss.

Mother Versus Daughter

Sadly, sometimes mothers and daughters are not able to recognise one another's needs. This may be because a mother is overwhelmed by the loss she has suffered and unable to recognise that her daughter has also suffered a major bereavement. Or, a daughter may feel that she has lost more than her mother has: perhaps because of real or imaginary difficulties between parents, or because she feels that the relationship between herself and her father was more important than the one that existed between her father and her mother.

If such conflicts emerge after the father's death, it usually means that they have been going on beneath the surface of that family's life for a long time. In such cases it would be wise for both mother and daughter to look outside the family for individual sources of support and comfort.

The Continuing Loss

The death of a father can affect so much in life. It can mean that our children lose a grandfather. If they are not yet born, then they will never have a chance to know him just as he will never have the opportunity of holding his grandchildren.

If we are not married, then we may lose the man who would have been at our wedding and played such an important part in that ceremony.

The loss of our father may upset the delicate balance of the other relationships in our life, perhaps with our mother or with our husband or boyfriend.

It is only through the process of time that we will discover the full implications of such a major bereavement.

A SON LOSES A FATHER

The relationship between father and son changes and develops over the years. It will be influenced by the personality of the two men - the differences and similarities of their interests. How father and son get on is also determined by the part mother plays in the family and how the men compete for her interest and attention. A son's need to rebel and the older man's need to be 'in control' of his family will also affect how they relate.

The father's death can happen at any stage; perhaps in the middle of a period of quarrels and confrontation, or when, at last, a real understanding has developed between father and son.

My Father My Friend

Some sons share a close bond with their father, and to lose their father is to lose the closest friend they have. There can be no substitute for such a loss. The world becomes a less secure and a less than perfect place, because the love, knowledge and companionship that was part of that father-son relationship is no longer there.

Loss Of The Man

The loss of the father can put a burden on a young man. A son may be expected to take on his father's various duties and functions. These can range from practical tasks, such as becoming the family driver, or the family form filler-in, or mechanic, to being put 'in charge' of the family group.

The Stiff Upper Lip

Men, young and old, are not supposed to show their feelings. However hurt they may be inside, it is expected that they somehow keep a stiff upper lip and support the more emotional females around them.

There are signs that, at long last, these simplistic generalisations about male and female behaviour are beginning to disappear. Just as women are now increasingly expected to take on work and skills previously reserved for men, so men are laying claim to those characteristics long seen as female. Men do have feelings and have as much right to express those feelings as women.

It can take courage to admit that one can't cope, that things are too difficult, that everything seems in a mess both inside oneself and in the world around us.

Living Up To An Ideal

Many sons try very hard to live up to the standards and ideals set by their father. Sometimes picking up the challenge to succeed brings unexpected success and knowing that a particular achievement would have pleased our father can bring a glow of satisfaction. Our achievements can seem to give our father's life and his death a very real meaning.

Dead Fathers Can't Change

A father, determined that his new-born son follow him into the family business, will, in all probability recognise this as a totally wrong career for his son by the time he reaches his teens.

The premature death of the father may sometimes persuade the family to go on trying for years to fulfil the father's wishes - much to the detriment of the young man. It is important to hold onto the fact that a dead father, unlike a living one, has no opportunity to change and develop his views.

Parents may seem unchangeable but they are not. They develop and grow along with their children.

Outliving Father

Some men find the period in their life when they reach the age their father was when he died has particular significance for them. It can be a point when, once again they recognise the loss they suffered years before, and once again they face thoughts of their own mortality.

THE DEATH OF A MOTHER

Perhaps no one has more influence over the developing child than its mother. It is from its mother's body that a child actually emerges; it is mother who will feed a child, either from her breast or by bottle - holding the infant close to her. It is a mother who will see to its daily needs for food, warmth, cleanliness and love.

Inspite of changing attitudes towards parenting in this country, surveys indicate that it is still the mother in the family who will do the majority of that feeding and bathing and nurturing which children need if they are to grow up into healthy adulthood.

Homemaker

It is generally mother who will be in charge of the home, and see that it is run efficiently for the whole family. It is she who ensures that there is food in the fridge, powder for the washing machine and curtains at the windows.

Educationalist

It is more likely to be mothers who attend school open-evenings. Who urge their children to do their homework, who discuss with them their hopes and plans for the future.

The Family Peace-Maker

Mothers may also have to be the peace-makers in a family, both between brothers and sisters, and between a father and his children.

When a family no longer has a peace-maker, arguments and rows break out; especially in those early months of bereavement when everyone is hurt and trying to cope with so much loss and change.

Now there is no-one to calm things down, or attempt to see both sides. Such a family is very vulnerable; for angry confrontations can result, all too often, in older children walking out, or even being thrown out. So much of the anger at this time really belongs to the bitterness and frustration that death brings with it. It is intensely sad if a family has to endure further loss. Sometimes more distant relatives or family friends can help, by temporarily acting as the peace-maker for a bereaved family.

Who Cares For Who?

It is generally mothers who care for their family. A family without a mother finds itself without a carer at the very time when they have the greatest need to be cared for. Who cares for who at such a time?

Little Children

Little children must be cared for physically and emotionally. Never more than now will they need love and continuity. Who will provide that love and security? Fathers are capable of mothering young children. It takes them time to learn a new set of skills, but men are as capable as women of providing a child with the love, attention and care it needs to grow up healthy and strong.

Even quite young children can contribute to the running of a home. They can learn to put their toys away when they have finished playing with them and help lay the table.

Older Children

The contribution that an older child may be expected to make to a family which has no mother is less clearly defined. Should an older girl (or boy) be expected to become a second 'mother' to younger children in the family, and perhaps in the process have to put her (or his) own needs to one side?

Just how much might an older child be expected to care for and support a grieving father? Obviously, these, and issues like them, should be talked over carefully before any decision is reached. It may be valuable to include other relatives and close family friends in such discussions. Their views may bring fresh insight, and, in listening, they may reach a new understanding of the problems the family is facing.

At The Centre Of The Larger Family

The mother usually acts as the link between the small nuclear family and the more extended one of aunts and uncles, cousins, and grandparents. Usually it is mothers who are best at remembering family birthdays, and arranging family gatherings.

Nurse And Comforter

When we think of a mother - a mother, not necessarily our mother - we think of someone who will look after us when we are ill. Someone who will hug us and make things better for us. To *mother* someone is to actively care for a person and supervise all their physical needs for food and comfort.

The Loss Of Mothering

To lose a mother is to lose the person who cared for us in that very special fashion. To lose a mother means that no one will ever*mother* us in precisely that way again; there will be no one to tell us to stop being lazy, to take off our shoes, change our underwear, eat properly, write our thank-you letters, and remember family anniversaries.

Alongside the actual person we have lost, we will also grieve for the loss of mothering itself. It may be years since our mother last nursed us or kissed us better, but, like a small child, something inside us will cry out for the loss of that love, and for a while the world may seem a colder and harder place because of the absence of it.

When we lose our mother we lose the person who has been an essential part of our life since we were born.

The Perfect Mother

The perfect mother will love her child unconditionally. However badly behaved it may be - whether or not a child leaves or remains at home - mother will always be there offering comfort and love, through thick and thin, through arguments and anger.

All of us have such a picture of a perfect mother in our minds. Perhaps this will have been made up from distant memories from when we were a little child, or from other people's mothers, or from stories we have read. It may be that our own mother was the perfect mother in every way, or, it may be that she never was that fairy-story kind of mother. She may well have been a 'modern' mother, with all the pressures of a full-time job, pushing meals into a microwave oven when she returned home from work, tired at the end of the day. She may have had other commitments, which meant that she had only a limited time to spend with her family.

The Good-Enough Mother

The woman who mothered her children so well when they were little and dependent on her, may find it hard to adapt to the demands of older children as they fight their way towards independence and the establishment of their own lives outside the family home. The borderline between caring and nagging, between discipline and domination can be finely drawn. It may not be possible to be a perfect mother to children in late adolescence. All one can be is a good-enough mother; responding in a good-enough way to the ever changing needs of good-enough children.

When The Death Happens

If we are between the ages of eighteen and twenty eight our mother will not have been very old when she died - probably no more than sixty. In a country where the life expectation for women is well into their seventies, such a death is experienced as premature and untimely. The younger we are the greater our sense of being robbed of our future with our mother. There will be no mother to cry at our wedding, or await the birth of her grandchild. No mother to turn to later in life when we might need a steadying hand.

Still At Home

If we are still living at home when our mother dies, then we will be living in a home which is dominated emotionally and physically by the the effects of her death.

It is likely that many of the routines of daily life will be altered. A major part of the family has been snatched from it, and, however hard everyone struggles to make do and share the tasks that are left undone, they will not be able to fill that huge space which has opened up in the home.

After an initial sense of unity the family may find itself stressed and overburdened as it tries to cope with each individual member's private grief and that multitude of new tasks confronting it.

Living Away

If we are living away from our home when our mother dies, her death may have less impact on our day-to-day life. Once the funeral is over, our daily routines go on much the same as they did before.

Because our lives are not so closely interlaced with those of our parents, people around us may assume that the loss has very little significance. Apart from an initial word of condolence, they may ignore our bereavement or expect us to have got over it in only a few weeks.

We too may expect ourselves to be more or less back to normal soon after the business of death has been dealt with. Living away, we may feel separate from the rest of the family, as if we don't really belong to it anymore and have not got the same rights to deep feelings as others still at home.

We may even be surprised at just how little we feel about our mother's death. Our thoughts may focus on our father if he is still alive, or on younger brothers or sisters, or other, more vulnerable relatives. Alternatively, we may find ourselves disturbed; lost and alone in a way we could never have anticipated.

Replacement Mothers

Statistically, men are more likely to re-marry or find a new partner after the death of their wife, than women are, after the death of their husband. Some men feel that they simply cannot live alone; that they need a woman in their life if they are to survive, and older men do have a higher rate of survival if they re-marry. Women are still the main emotional and physical carers in our society. It is hard for a man to get the support and love he needs from his own sex.

Many men feel that children need a mother, and, therefore, they have a duty to find a substitute mother-figure for their children. Some wives on their death-bed instruct their husbands to go out and find a new wife after their death.

Men tend to be problem-solvers, and often the solution to so many of their problems - loneliness, sadness, need for love and companionship - seems to lie in a new partnership.

It is not easy to find space for the work of grief when one is involved in the work of creating a new union. Grief involves looking backwards at the past and at everything that has been lost from life. New unions demand that we look forward with hope towards the formation of a new future.

It is all too easy for the needs of young, or not-so-young children to get lost at such a time. At a point when they are still grieving, they may be asked to move forward with their father, to delight in his happiness. They may be told it is morbid and unhealthy to dwell on the past. Caught between their fathers needs and their own, they may feel angry and confused. Time usually solves such difficulties - meanwhile, there may be a need for the children to find an outside source of support and understanding.

Where real differences emerge, a relative or close family friend may be able to mediate between child and parent. This should preferably be someone who can remain reasonably neutral; able to see that both sides have their own particular needs and point of view.

No one can take the place of someone we love. People are not interchangeable. If a father marries again we will acquire a step-mother and not a mother. That step-mother may or may not be able to mother us. Much will depend on her and on us.

Somehow, we have to find a balance between the needs of the past and the needs of the present and future. We may also have to balance our personal needs against those of other members of our family, needs which may be very different from our own.

A DAUGHTER LOSES A MOTHER

On the whole it is our mother who nurtures and cares for us - although in families without a mother, a father, grandparent, older sister, aunt or foster parent may take over that mothering role.

In most families the skills of mothering are passed on from generation to generation. Daughters are enabled to become good mothers because of the good mothering they have received. There may have been no conscious learning process, but somehow, the ability to care for a home and family has been learnt.

When a daughter loses a mother, the chain that links the genera-tions is broken, and a special kind of loss is experienced.

Best Friends

Some mothers and daughters are very close to one another. The daughter recognises that in their mother they have a continuing source of knowledge and care. The two women can join together to create a strong and very successful union. Such women truly say of one another that, besides being mother and daughter, they are also 'best friends'.

Best friends share problems. Best friends are always there when we need them. Best friends care for us and think of us as very special people.

When the mother dies, the daughter finds that besides losing her mother she also faces the loss of her best friend. Now there is no-one with that special understanding; no-one to go shopping with and help search out the things that really suit us, no-one to discuss the merits and demerits of past or future boy friends, no-one to commiserate with us, or share our joys.

Motherless Mothers

Daughters often go on to become the carers in their new families; taking on the feeding and nurturing of their babies and looking after their husbands or partners. It can be hard to carry on being a mother if one suddenly has no mother oneself.

When we are grieving it can be difficult to find the energy and strength necessary to mother those who are dependent upon us.

Many people do not understand the full implications of the loss of a mother. They may think that although it's sad to lose a mother, it isn't the end of the world. After all, there are all those other people needing and loving us, so, what is all the fuss about?

Husbands Get Anxious

A husband may worry that his wife is grieving too much after the death of her mother; that her grief seems to be getting out of control. He may be frightened that the children will be neglected and he may be feeling very neglected himself. Helpless to change things, he watches his wife struggle to try to come to terms with the great loss she has suffered.

A major bereavement can place a great strain on relationships between a young husband and wife, especially in the first year of bereavement.

Difficult Mothers

It is not unusual for daughters and mothers to clash in those fraught teenage years; and, further, to go on clashing for some time.

Sometimes the relationship will improve once a daughter establishes her own home, her own personal territory away from her parents. Sometimes it improves when she has children of her own.

Sometimes, however, we are not given the opportunity for improvement. Our mother dies before we have had a chance to learn and to understand why she acted as she did - and why we needed to act as we did.

Death destroys any chance of reconciliation. It also takes away our chance of putting our point of view or of expressing the anger we may still be feeling.

Bad Mothering

If our mother was a bad mother, how can we ever be a good mother ourselves?

After a death, we often concentrate on the time just before the death. It is easy to forget that the relationship we have lost has a far longer history. We may have had wonderful mothering in those early, important, formative years of our life, and this will not have been wasted - whatever the difficulties of subsequent years. Locked within us, is that earlier experience of being mothered well. We draw upon that experience, even when we cannot really remember it.

Into The Future

Good or bad, our mother plays a very important part in our lives. Her influence on our past and our present is considerable, and she will continue to influence us after her death. We will go on monitoring ourselves, measuring ourselves against the standards she set; whether or not we chose to rebel against those standards, or live our life by similar rules.

There will be times when we are glad that our mother is not there to see a particular mess we have made. There will also be times when we wish our mother had lived to see our successes.

Guardian Angels

For a daughter, it is her mother who stands as the guardian between herself and her own approaching death. As long a mother is alive thoughts of mortality can be put to one side. When a daughter's mother dies, there is the sudden realisation that it is her turn next. It may be several decades before that death comes, but for a while it can feel very close indeed.

A SON LOSES A MOTHER

The relationship between mother and son is an important one. It is through his mother that a son first learns about the world. Like his baby sister, he is kissed, cuddled, bathed, fed and cared for. But this period of physical mothering can be short lived, because boys are often expected to grow up faster than girls - to control their emotions and become young men.

Touching And Feeling

Until he reaches an age when he begins to connect up with girls, a boy's mother may be his only link with women, and through her with the world of emotions and the senses. She may be the only one allowed to express her feelings for him, brush his hair, hold his hand, acknowledge that he might want to cry if something hurts him. She may be the only one who understands that quite big boys need to cry sometimes.

No Mum, No Mothering

Fathers, friends and other relatives may be able to provide some of this particular kind of mothering, but sometimes, until a son joins up with another woman able to love him and let him love her, he may be without this nurturing, touching motherly love.

Unconditional Love

Ideally, a mother will love her son unconditionally, and, when she dies, there is no-one who can ever love in quite that way again. In reality this may be far from the truth but we grieve for the loss of that ideal.

Even a man's wife cannot substitute totally for his mother, because the relationship between husband and wife is based on equality and is also conditional on good behaviour and obeying certain rules.

Good And Bad Mothers

The premature death of a very good mother may leave us feeling bitter. Why should such a person die?

Unless one has the amazing good fortune to have had a 'perfect mother', it is likely that our mother will have been both 'good and bad', at one time or another, throughout our upbringing. The death of a 'bad' mother will create difficult and distressing feelings. All hope of reconciliation or change will be destroyed by the death. It is not that we will *not* grieve such a loss, but that we will also need to grieve for the previous loss of the good mothering we may have received in the past.

Bringing Back The Child

The death of our mother may make us feel like a child once again - vulnerable, exposed and needy.

Her death may also give us a sense of real release and freedom from parental control.

Both feelings are hard to cope with. As a man, there may be no-one prepared to listen to us if we do try and describe how we are feeling.

As a man we may be expected to control our feelings, especially in public. We may also be expected to look after other people; our grieving father or younger brothers and sisters. It can be hard to look after others when we are feeling hurt and lost ourselves.

Problem-Solving

Perhaps men more than women are taught to be solvers of problems, to look for the solution which will put things right. There is no solution to grief. Grief is an experience that has to be lived through. Grief is not the enemy that must, at all costs, be kept at bay, it is a correct and natural response to loss by death.

The Loss Of A Creator

When a son loses a mother, he loses part of his history. He loses the person who has played a major part in the creation of the person he is and has become. He loses a unique relationship, and his feelings after that loss will also be unique.

BECOMING AN ORPHAN

To be orphaned is to have lost both parents through death. It is not just little children that become orphaned. We can become an orphan when we are six or 66. Whatever our age, we have to confront the fact that we are now living in a world in which we have no parents at all.

Such a fact of life has consequences. There is no-one automatically responsible for us any longer; no longer anyone who will care for us, for no other reason than the fact that we are their child. On the other hand, there is no parent able to make a claim on us; no-one to care for in their old age and infirmity. A set of mutual obligations has been ended for ever.

The End Of Childhood

The death of our parents completes our childhood even though we may still technically be a child. It also brings to an end one part of our life.

The Loss Of Our History

It may be many years before we are able to look back at our past and start to investigate it once again.

Our parents retain the memories of our infancy and childhood in their minds. When they die they take those memories with them. There may be no-one now who knows what time of day it was when we were born, or whether or not we were breast-fed. No-one to answer a thousand little questions we should wish to have answered. Sometimes, though, if we are lucky, other family members can help fill in those gaps in our knowledge.

Nothing Left To Lose

If we are not yet established in long-term committed relationships, then the sense of not really belonging anywhere can be frightening at times. We may be free from parental pressure, but, freedom, in the words of a well-known pop song, can be, "just another word for nothing left to lose."

Two Major Bereavements

In order to become an orphan we will have had to survive the impact of two major bereavements. If we are still in our late teens or early adult years we will have had to face death and confront deep grief at a relatively early stage in our life.

Each of those losses will hold a special significance and meaning for us. Each will have its own history and will have created its own set of feelings and reactions within us.

Being Different

We do not expect to be made an orphan in our late teens, or even in our twenties. And, if we do lose our parents at such a time, it is unlikely we will know others in a similar situation. We become different from our friends and colleagues because of the special loss that we have suffered. How could they, who have parents, possibly understand what it is like to find oneself so alone in life?

We exist in a world where others are frequently discussing their parents; perhaps moaning about them, or making the assumption that a parent is there to baby-sit or pay for the wedding, or want us there at Christmas time.

For those that have living parents it is hard to imagine what life would be like without them. Until we lose our parents, we make the assumption that they will always be there somewhere in the background of our life. It is not until they have gone for ever that we are able to acknowledge their importance, and feel the gap they leave behind them.

Different Ways Of Becoming An Orphan

Our first parent may have died many years ago, perhaps when we were a baby or toddler. Our remaining parent having been left to take on the sole responsibility for our up-bringing. The later death of that single parent will leave us absolutely alone.

Alternatively, we may have lost our first parent within the last few years. The loss of our second parent may bring back the emotions we experienced at that time; and, unexpectedly, we may find ourselves grieving two bereavements.

Or, we may have only recently lost our first parent. Perhaps it was that death which directly - or indirectly - led to this loss of our second parent. The stress and strain of being widowed can cause ill health, and it can be hard to find reasons to go on in those first painful years. Still shocked by the first loss we find ourselves confronting this second one.

Sometimes parents die together; perhaps in an accident or disaster. These abrupt endings create great shock. Our life is utterly changed, with no warning or opportunity for any kind of preparation.

Practical Implications

The death of our second and last parent is far more likely to expose us to the world of wills, probate, solicitors, insurance companies, financial problems and complications over inheritance of property or money.

It may possibly mean the clearance and sale of the family home, and the question of where we will live.

If there are younger brothers and sisters, their needs will have to be taken into consideration. Will it be possible to keep the remaining family together? Questions of guardianship may have to be resolved. There will be careful thought needed before long-term decisions are made.

Getting Advice

To be orphaned often necessitates the need for large practical changes to be made in one's daily life. It is important that one has clear and impartial practical and financial advice in the early months of one's bereavement.

Act First, Feel Later

The actual business of death can 'take us over' in the first weeks and months of our loss, and only later do we find ourselves confronting the emotional impact of the loss we have suffered; the questioning, the anger, the feeling of being suddenly alone.

Having people around us who will listen to us when we need to talk, who will tolerate our changes of mood and help us to see that we are not going mad but doing the intensely painful and complex work of grief will help in this difficult period. Well-meaning, but unwanted advice - from whatever source - can increase a sense of confusion; and great patience may well be needed. Good listeners can be invaluable at such a time. Support and understanding can come from a wide variety of sources. Usually people are only too willing to try and help but anxious that if they bring up the subject of our loss they may be intruding on our privacy or make things worse.

The Effects Of Our Grief On Those We Love

If we are married or living with someone, then it is quite possible that such a large happening in our life will affect the relationship between us and our partner.

The crisis we are going through may strengthen the bond between us, drawing us together in mutual support. It may equally place a severe strain on the relationship for quite a long time. Intense grief changes us. We need to think at a deep level. We may need to re-assess who we are and where we are going in life.

We may not understand our changes of mood and emotion from day to day, and these will be even less understandable to our partners.

They may be forced into a situation where they long to reach out and help us, but do not know how best to do so.

Carrying On

What we have had in the past and what we have lost will be carried with us into our present and our future life. Such a major bereavement as the death of our parents must have an effect on us for as long as we live.

However, unbelievable as it seems in the black, early days of loss, people do learn to live without parents. They go on to build new routines and learn to enjoy their lives; they make successful relationships, work hard, and in turn eventually become parents to their own children.

THE DEATH OF A BROTHER OR SISTER

To lose a sister or a brother is to lose one of the most important people in our lives.

We grow up alongside our brothers and our sisters. They are a part of our history. They are irreplaceable.

Apart from our parents, no-one will have greater influence over the formation of our character and the person we are than our siblings - our brothers and sisters.

The Only One

If we lose our only brother or sister in our teens or twenties then we lose a unique relationship. We will probably never be a brother or a sister to anyone again. No-one will call us 'sis' or 'bro'. With the person who died has ended a very important relationship and a role that we have played for most of our life.

Our Place In The Family

There is research that indicates that the place we have as a child in a family will affect the development of certain skills; for example, first children are likely to learn to read quicker than second or subsequent children.

The fact that we have a brother or a sister is important, and the fact that we are the eldest in our family, or the middle child, or the youngest, or come from a large family - that too, will influence how we are defined by our parents and how we learn to see ourselves within the context of our family group.

When a brother or sister dies, our place within our family group is affected. If our elder brother dies and we become the oldest child in the family, then certain things may be expected of us. And yet it is impossible to step into that space left by his death. The skills and special characteristics he possessed are not easily appropriated by other family members.

Parents Define Children

Parents start defining their children from the moment they are born.

"She was always a good baby - no trouble at all."

"He kept me awake all night - a real terror."

If a first child is seen as bright and quick, the second might have to be the sensitive, thoughtful one.

By the time parents reach a third child they are more confident and relaxed as parents, and so these children are often more confident too. There is less pressure on them to have to succeed and prove their parents successful.

Competition

Being a child within a family involves competition. Children naturally compete for their parents' love and attention. We all long to be the most loved and most important child. Most rows between children are because of this need to have proved their place in the family.

Some parents are better than others at dealing with all this competition. Some deny that it exists. They say they love all their children exactly the same. In truth, although they probably do love all of their children very deeply indeed - they do so in different ways. What they often find difficult to express is that their *liking* for their children changes from time to time. Children go through stages where they are argumentative, rude and need to confront the rules of the family. It is very hard for some parents to demonstrate equality of affection throughout such difficult periods.

Having Favourites

In some families there are clear allegiances formed, and it is acknowledged that dad and his daughter get on best, or that mum and her son have a special relationship, or the other way around - "She's her mother's daughter." Sometimes one particular child is seen by everyone to be 'the special one'. This may be because they are especially sensitive or especially clever, or because they have a disability or illness - which means they are perceived as having developed special qualities - or are in need of special care.

Becoming The Special One

The child who dies becomes the 'special child' within the family. Everything that the child has done, or thought, or been acquires a very special significance because of their death.

The Wrong Child Died

Because of this natural need to concentrate on the 'specialness' of the child who has died, the remaining children can be made to feel that perhaps it was the wrong child who died - that it would be better if they had died instead.

They may feel that they can never hope to live up to the 'specialness' of their dead sister or brother. However successful they become, however much they love their parents, or do the right thing, they can never make up for the loss. It can be extremely hard to grow up in the shadow of a dead child.

Over-Protective Parents

Parents who have lost one child may live in fear of losing their other children. This is particularly true if the death was sudden and unexpected. The world becomes that much more dangerous. The other children in the family may find that all their actions are carefully overseen, that it is no longer alright to come back late from parties, or ride on motor-bikes, or travel in a friend's car.

My Loss/My Grief

It is all too easy for a young person's grief over the loss of a brother or a sister to get swallowed up in the loss their parents have suffered. The focus of attention and support can be firmly fixed on the parents, and especially on the mother. There may be little acknowledgement that children in the family will also be devastated by the loss they have suffered.

It may be assumed that the remaining children's role has to be one of support to their parents. At a time when we most need looking after ourselves, it seems that we are expected to look after our parents - not only is a precious sister or brother lost, but at the same time one appears to lose one's parents as well.

Family Grief

Many families do join together in their sadness, especially in the early days and weeks of loss. Some, however, find it hard to share their thoughts and feelings. This is understandable because each individual is grieving alone for the unique loss they have suffered. Each will set their own pace within the grieving process; their own need to speak or remain silent, to cry or find comfort in laughter with friends.

My Sister/My Brother

The death of a brother or sister will change us. For a while we will exist as part of a grieving family, and this will form a marked contrast to the world outside our home where life is going on much as it did before the death.

Getting away from the family's sadness and tears can be important as it allows us the space to think and feel our own thoughts. It can take a long time to work out what it is that we have lost and the effects that loss will have on us and our life.

This understanding of our personal loss is part of the hard work of grief. It does not go on all the time. It comes and goes. We will have periods when we need to think of the past, and periods when the present and the future dominate our thoughts.

My Friend

Very often our brother or sister is our closest ally and our best friend. The world can seem a lonelier place when that friendship has disappeared.

How And Why

Some deaths are harder to understand than others. It is hard to accept that a brother or sister could have chosen to take their own life. It is hard to accept that their life could have been ended so wastefully, perhaps by someone's carelessness - a driving accident, or failure to observe proper rules. Again, it is hard to accept that a young life can be cut short by illness.

The death of any young person is never easy to understand. It challenges our ideas of rightness and wrongness in life.

Death Has To Have A Meaning

At some point we need to believe that the death had some kind of purpose - that it wasn't just a meaningless ending to a young life.

We have also to believe that our brother or sister's life had some meaning and purpose to it, even though it was far shorter than it should have been.

Perhaps it is through the exploration of the meaning of life and death that mankind progresses. The death of someone we love forces us to confront this major philosophical issue.

The Empty Place

The death of a member of a family leaves an empty place within that group. Even when the pain of grief is past and life once again begins to go on in a regular fashion, there can be a continuing sense that something is missing.

Of course, it is *someone* who is missing. Someone very near - someone with similar genes, someone close in age, someone who had a share in our growing-up.

There will be times when the loss seems particularly significant; those occasions where, if they had been alive, our brother or sister would have had a part to play. They would have delighted with us at the new baby, cried with us at a family funeral, laughed at us for being ridiculous, been there when we needed them.

A DEATH IN ONE'S NEW FAMILY

Being young or relatively young offers no automatic protection against death. Sadly, in spite of all mankind's advancement in knowledge and skill over the past decades, it is still possible to lose those we love when they are still a very long way off old age.

The bereavements we may suffer in our new marriages and unions are most likely to involve the untimely death of a young person; a young husband or wife, a baby or a child. These tragic losses are different from those occurring within our parental family.

However painful and shattering the deaths of our grandparents, or even our parents, at least they are part of the normal order and pattern of life. Ultimately, we will be able to see that the loss of those who helped in the creation of the person we have become is an important stage in the process of our own maturation.

Deaths occurring when we are young, in our own generation, or the generation below us, affect the new units and relationships we are in the very process of creating. These premature deaths end not only the present, but also rob us of our future.

THE DEATH OF A PARTNER

Somewhere in the decade which stretches from late teens to late twenties the majority of young people in this country chose that special person who will become their life partner - the person with whom they decide to share their future.

For some, the decision will have been taken in their teens, and, by the time they reach the end of their twenties, they will have been married for some years. They may be well on their way to completing their family group at an age when others will be just beginning to set up home together.

Although there is evidence that young people are delaying marriage until a later age, marriage, as an institution, has not lost its popularity. People still meet, fall in love and get married. Many of those whose first marriages fail, still go on to marry again.

Some young couples chose to live together as man and wife. Although not undertaking the legal commitment of marriage, they create an on-going partnership and one which may possibly include children. Long-term committed partnerships are also created by gay men and lesbian women.

Inside or outside marriage, such couples are bound together by the strength of the continuing commitment they have made to one another. To lose a partner through death shatters the life they have built together, and destroys the future they were in the process of creating.

Straight Into The Business Of Death

The younger one is, and the less established one's relationship, the greater the influence from outside might be, in the making of those important decisions about where, when and how the funeral should take place. There may hardly be time to take in the fact that the death has happened before being confronted with the need to make decisions on a wide range of practical matters. It can help to know one's rights, right from the beginning.

Next Of Kin

If the partnership has been legalised by marriage, then the remaining partner will automatically be defined as the next of kin of the one who has died. This will give them certain rights over the arrangements surrounding the burial of the body. They may also have legal rights on the estate, and to be entitled to certain state benefits.

No Legal Contract

If there has been no marriage and no legal provision made in case of death, then it can be surprisingly difficult to claim rights over the ceremony, money, property and even grief.

Common-law partners can find they have far fewer rights than they thought.

Both heterosexual and homosexual partners can find the importance of the part they played in the life of the one they have lost minimised by the relatives of the deceased. Perhaps because of ignorance, or because it was viewed as an unacceptable partnership by the family.

When one has loved and shared one's life with someone for any length of time, it can be very hard indeed to find oneself excluded from the planning of those ceremonies surrounding their death.

The Funeral

One of the rights and duties of the next of kin is to arrange and organise the funeral proceedings. Obviously, in most families this would be done in discussion with other important family members, and there is normally no dispute over how and where the service should be carried out.

Occasionally, disputes do arise, especially where the relationship between the partners was unclear, or troubled, or very short. In such cases, the parents or family of the person who has died may feel they have greater rights over the deceased. The law states that the body can only be released to the person who is technically the next of kin to the deceased, who then has an obligation and a right to ensure that it is suitably dealt with.

A Difference Of Size

There can be a great deal of difference between the funeral of an elderly person and that of a young man or woman in the very prime of their life.

An elderly person may well have lost the majority of their friends and relatives through death already; and it is likely that only the younger generations will attend the funeral, plus, perhaps, one or two remaining close friends and neighbours.

A younger person may have links with many different groups. There may be school and college friends who are still in touch, and work colleagues and new friends, as well as relatives from both sides of the family. Such a large gathering reflects the deep loss that such a premature death brings in its wake.

Until Death Us Do Part

People do not enter marriage lightly (in spite of the present high divorce rate); they make a promise - a contract for life - which at the time, they have every intention of keeping. The expiry date on that contract is the death of one or other of the partners.

Unless we marry someone knowing that they have a very serious illness or terminal disability, we do not expect our partners to die young. We expect them to live for many, many years; just as we expect to still be alive to see our children grow up and produce children of their own.

Not An Easy Death

On the whole, the young do not easily give up their right to life. They have too much to live for. It takes a very serious illness, an act of violence or abnormal circumstances to release their hold on life.

Not A Usual Death

Once, not so long ago, many mothers died in childbirth. Once, it was not uncommon for thousands of young men to be killed in war. Once, plague and cholera accounted for the death of many who were still young. Today, it is unusual to lose a young partner through death. Those who are bereaved at an early stage in their marriage know themselves to be an exception to the general rule. They recognise that their bereavement marks them out as different from those around them.

Because the situation of losing a young partner though death is relatively rare, people do not know how to respond to it. In our society there is no clear set of rules which define how a young widow or widower should behave in the days and months following their bereavement, and none defining the kind of help and support they might expect from their friends and family.

No-One To Live With

The death of a partner is a major bereavement; its effects will be felt in nearly all aspects of daily life for a long time. It is a bereavement which encompasses an enormous range of loss.

The death of our partner leaves us very alone indeed. There is no-one there now in the morning when we wake up, no-one to greet us in the evening at the end of the working day. The loss of the person we have chosen to share our life will affect every day of the rest of our life. We have to learn how to fill the vacuum left by their going. We have to learn to live all over again and this process of re-structuring our lives can take many months.

No-One To Sleep With

Most couples share a bed. It can be hard to learn to sleep alone, especially in the early days of grief when sleep is so often disturbed. There is no-one now to cuddle up to in the night, no-one to reach out to for warmth and comfort.

No-One To Make Love With

One of the reasons why people chose to share their lives together is because they love one another physically as well as emotionally and intellectually.

The loss of someone to love, to touch, to physically hold, and have intercourse with, is a very great loss indeed. There is no immediate solution to such a loss.

The need to be held, to love and be loved can be overwhelming in the early months of bereavement; but new relationships do not always mix easily with intense grief and, if one has been used to a long-term committed relationship it can be hard to adjust to shorter less meaningful affairs.

Bereaved men and women can be shocked to find that they continue to have sexual desires in the weeks and months following the death of their partner. Knowing that such feelings are perfectly natural does not make it any easier to deal with the situation, but might take away some of the pressure and guilt that such feelings can generate.

It is just as 'normal' to have no sexual urges at this time, the numbing effects of the shock of death can keep these inclinations submerged for quite a long time. This does not mean one has become impotent, or sexless for the rest of one's life; only that it is necessary to put up defences for a while against some of the pain of loss.

The Loss Of A Home

Sometimes, money may well be the least of one's problems when one has just lost a dearly loved partner, and indeed, many young widows and widowers find that, once they have sorted our their affairs, they are able to live on without too many financial anxieties (this is especially true if the partner's life was covered by an insurance policy). Knowing that longed-for financial security has been achieved at such a high cost can create intense feelings of guilt.

Other people find that their partner's death means that they are unable to carry on living in their present home. Young people's budgets are often stretched to the very limit. If there are no children, both partners may be working. Even so, there might only be just enough to pay the rent or mortgage with nothing at all left over for emergencies or savings. At a time when there is most need for stability and continuity, losing one of those precious incomes can threaten everything.

Going Backwards

Caring parents may offer the comfort and support so needed at this time of deep sadness, and there may be much sense in going back home to be looked after - even if only for a while. However, it can be hard to return back to being a child in the household having been part of a relationship where one existed as a equal adult partner. Whilst longing for that comfort and support we get from our parents we may find it hard to accept the restrictions that being treated as a child brings with it.

The newer and less established the relationship ended by death, the more we may be encouraged to forget it, to put it out of our minds, and move either back to the point we were at before it happened, or onwards to a new relationship.

Of course it is impossible to deny the past, and it is important that we have time to stay with our sadness, to recognise what it is we have lost, and grieve for that loss before moving on into the future.

Who Am I Anyway?

The death of someone we love forces us to re-assess who we are. The death of a partner destroys a relationship; a role we have held in life is taken away from us. In the eyes of the world, we are no longer a husband, or a wife, or one of a partnership.

The death of our partner means we have become a 'single' person once again. However, in the early days of grief we do not feel single. We may feel closer to our partner than we have ever done before. The work of grief concentrates our thoughts and minds on the one we have lost. The emotional state of grief is very close to that of being 'in love'.

We are alone, and yet our mind is full of the ones we have lost We are bound tightly into a relationship that exists in our mind, but not on this earth.

We are a grieving person; perhaps this is the role that we have to hold onto at this intensely difficult time of our life. Eventually, new roles will open up to us, and, once again, we will have a clearer idea of who we are.

What About The Children?

If the partnership included children then their needs will continue, however sad and distressed we may feel. The work of caring for them goes on inspite of our loss.

"At least you have the children," - is a remark often made and intended to comfort the young man or woman who has lost their partner. And children can, by their very demands, force us to go on at a time when we might often feel like giving it all up. Children can give life back its meaning and purpose when, in those bleak early months of bereavement, it seems to have almost disappeared.

But however much we may love our children, they are no substitute for the love of a partner. When we are grieving deeply it can be so hard to find love inside ourselves for anyone, even our own children.

Of course, they too will be grieving. Even little children are aware that things change; that someone important is no longer there - that there is sadness in the home. They may not be able to express their confusion and fears in words, and their grief may come out in their behaviour; perhaps in wetting the bed, or needing to cling for safety to their remaining parent.

Bringing Them Up Alone

The prospect of bringing children up alone without a partner's support can seem a frightening one, especially in the early days of loss.

How can boys grow up without a dad to guide them into manhood? How can a man bring his little daughter up without a mother there to provide the mothering she so much needs?

Although it is intensely hard to be a lone parent, a comforting truth is that children do thrive successfully in single-parent households. They do grow up to be normal and healthy and strong. Of course, they can be deprived of many of the things they would have had if their other parent had survived, but thousands of single parents have proved that it is possible to be both 'mum' and 'dad' to their children.

The Loss Of The Future

To lose one's life partner when young is to lose the very future one is in the process of creating. All the hopes and dreams and plans for the years ahead are suddenly shattered. It is to lose the baby that one was planning to have next year. It is to lose growing old, and the opportunity of retiring together. The list of potential loss goes on and on. It is not fair to lose a partner when one is young with so much that still needs to be said and done. It is no wonder that there are times when one screams aloud at the total unfairness of it all.

THE DEATH OF A CHILD

No Death So Sad is the title of a leaflet produced by The Compassionate Friends, the self-help organisation run by and for parents who have lost a child through death - and perhaps there is no death which affects all of us as deeply as that of a child.

Do Little Children Die Of It?

Do little children die of it? - is a question which can be used as a universal method of separating the really important issues in life from those which are less important. It is the yardstick for all societies, for, if little children do die of it, whether *it* be pollution, illness, famine, accident or war, then something somewhere is seriously wrong.

Just as we, as parents assume a degree of responsibility for the safety of our children, so society also accepts that it has a major role to play in the protection of these, its youngest and most vulnerable members.

Sadly, even in a peaceful basically caring and knowledgeable society such as ours, little children do continue to die. We have not yet found a way of protecting our young from accidental death both inside the home and outside it, and perhaps we never will. The cost of perfect safety, if such a state existed, would be too high in terms of lack of freedom and in the chance to explore, what is after all, a far-from-safe world. And, inspite of the vast increase in our medical knowledge, there are still diseases that claim the lives of our children, however desperately we search for prevention and cure.

The 'All Wrong' Death

Our children are our future; they are supposed to outlive us. The natural pattern of life is that the old give way to the young. It is sad, but natural to lose through death an elderly person, it is intensely sad and unnatural to lose a child.

We do not expect our children to die. As a parent, everything within us is geared to preserving our children's lives. From the moment they are born we assume the task of taking care of them - when they are hungry we feed them, when they cry we comfort them, the money we earn goes towards their well being, when they are ill we nurse them until they are better.

Part of the role of parenting is to ensure that our children are brought up in a safe environment and that they are protected against the dangers of the outside world.

There are some things which are beyond our control, and, inspite of all our love and care, our children may still die. If they do, our feelings of loss can be overwhelming. It is intensely hard to find a way of living on after the death of a dearly loved child, and as that child's parent, we may find ourself looking long and hard at the events surrounding the death, trying to understand how such a loss could have happened.

How Could The Death Have Been Prevented?
After the death of a child, society too will need to try and find the causes which lay behind that loss of life; because children are too precious to have them slip away.

The death will properly be investigated by experts. The parents of the child will also be conducting their own personal kind of investigation into the death. This may involve going over and over the events leading up to and surrounding it. Why did it happen? How could it have been prevented? What could they have done as a parent to stop their child dying? What can society do to ensure that no other child ever dies in the same way? How can we make this dangerous world a safer place for our children to grow up in?

Accidental Death
Part of learning to cope with life involves experiment. Children are great experimenters, they have to be, if they are to grow up strong and confident. But this very quality, essential for their well-being, often places them in some danger. A healthy adventurous child wants to climb to the top of the slide, and go on the swings, and jump off the wall, and wants to cross the road, and learn to ride a bike. All such activities involve an element of risk. Very, very occasionally an action which has been repeated perfectly safely a million times over by other children leads to a tragedy.

A Terrible Waste Of Life
When a child dies the whole of its future dies with it. It will never grow up and go on to have children of its own. It will never develop beyond the point it reached on the day it died. There is great poignancy in what appears to be such a senseless waste of life and potential.

How can we, as the child's parents, make sense out of what seems to be such a senseless loss? What possible meaning or purpose can there be in the death of a child?

These large and seemingly unanswerable questions confront many parents who lose a child.

Terminal Illness

As a society, we pride ourselves on the list of illnesses that we have conquered. Few now die of scarlet fever, or cholera or tuberculosis. Sadly, some illnesses and diseases are still beyond our ability to control. Our children can die of leukaemia, cystic fibrosis and heart disease - with many more waiting to steal our children from us.

Most of us hold onto the firm belief that we will recover from illness. If our children become ill, whilst we may worry about them, we do not expect them to die - we hold on to our trust in their survival.

Sometimes a child will accept that it is going to die long before its parents are able to reach the same conclusion; even though they have been given all the information about the seriousness of the situation by the doctors.

It is intensely hard to watch a child in pain or discomfort and know there is nothing we can do to ease their suffering. It can be almost impossible to accept the coming death of our child when everything in us fights for their preservation - when if it would help, we would even be prepared to sacrifice our own life for them.

Preparing For Death

If we are able to accept the inevitability of the ending, we may be able to help our child by sharing with them their fears and their thoughts about death and what they think will happen to them afterwards.

Children, like adults, need time to finish off the business of life, and to make their farewells properly. They can gain great comfort in knowing that their wishes for the funeral will be respected. Many children are deeply worried about their parents' inability to cope with their sadness. If this burden is taken from them, they are better able to face their own ending calmly and with dignity.

After The Loss

Parents who have lost a child after a long illness may be deeply exhausted; for many months their lives will have been focused on caring for their child. Now their child has gone there is nothing to care for any longer. It is as if the centre of the world has disappeared. No amount of preparation for the coming death will prevent the feeling of loss and loneliness felt when a life eventually ends.

If I Lose My Child Am I Still A Parent?

The death of those closest to us changes the role we play in life. If we lose our only child we are no longer the parent of a living child, and our lives will not automatically bring us alongside other parents; we will never collect a child up from school or take it to watch football matches.

We are a parent now to a child who has died. Our experience of being a child's parent will be with us for ever; no-one can take our past away from us.

"Do I say I have two children or three?"

This is something a parent may ask who has lost one of their children. When we are strong enough we may be able to say the truth, that we have three children but one of them is dead.

Other Children In The Family

The death of one of our children is such a huge event that it will consume us for a long time. It must also affect how we will treat any other children we may have. We may find that we cling onto them, afraid to let them out of our sight unless they too disappear.

Conversely our other children may seem insignificant compared to the child we have lost. Everything inside is screaming to hold the lost child once again, and one's surviving children cannot fill the gap. They too will be hurt, confused and grieving. Not only have they lost a brother or sister, but the very security of their world has been destroyed, and the people they expect to help - us - their parents, may be so overwhelmed by our own sadness that we find it impossible to take their pain alongside our own.

It is important that children are cared for at such a time; that they receive accurate and truthful information about what is happening, and that they know an adult is there to answer their questions and deal with their fears.

Dealing With A Partner's Grief

All of us grieve in very different ways for the personal loss that we have suffered. When we are absorbed with our own feelings it is hard to accept that other people have feelings too, and that those feelings are quite likely to be different from our own.

In many families who lose a child, the mother is seen as the main griever and the father takes on the role of trying to hold the family together. He may still have to go out to work each day if the family is to eat. He may wish to talk about his feelings, but find people reluctant to listen to him, or, he may find it impossible to describe what is going on inside his mind.

Sometimes, husbands and wives are able to share their feelings, but often they will be at different stages of grief at different times.

In the search to try and understand why the death happened, parents may find themselves blaming one another - If you hadn't gone away he wouldn't be dead! Why didn't you stay in that night? You never showed that you loved her!

There are a thousand ways to hurt someone at such a time, and, when one is so hurt oneself, the words just come tumbling out. The high separation and divorce rate amongst couples who have lost a child is evidence of the great difficulties parents confront at such a time.

Loss Without End

The effects of losing a child will last for ever. Most bereaved parents find that they keep a hidden calendar in their minds. The date when the child would have reached sixteen or twenty one, and birthdays and special days are all remembered.

Though it may return from time to time, deep grief will not always be present; and although life can never be the same with our child no longer there as part of it, we will learn to create and live a new life for ourselves and with those that we love.

Help

The Compassionate Friends (6 Denmark Street, Bristol, BS1 5DQ) is an organisation run by and for parents who have lost a child. They have contacts throughout the British Isles and may be able to put you in touch with someone in a similar situation.

They run a special group for parents who have lost a child through suicide and can also put parents of murdered children in touch with one another.

Talking with other bereaved parents can be invaluable but you might also wish to explore your thoughts and feelings with a bereavement counsellor. Your local Citizen Advice Bureau will be able to tell you if there is a local branch of Cruse or other bereavement service in your part of the country.

DEATH BEFORE BIRTH: MISCARRIAGE AND ABORTION

From the moment that we become aware of the pregnancy, and know for certain that we are to become the mother or the father of this unborn child we start to prepare ourselves and plan for that major event that lies ahead.

As far as the outside world is concerned, we may appear to be exactly the same as we always were. But, just as inside the mother's body great changes are taking place, so, inside her mind and that of the father of the child, a multitude of thoughts, feelings and ideas will be in progress.

Preparation For Parenthood

In later pregnancy, potential parents can attend classes designed to help them when it comes to giving birth to the baby. That is only one part of the preparation needed as we travel from the point of conception to the moment when we will hold our baby in our arms.

Mentally, we need to prepare ourselves for that change from prospective parenthood to actual parenthood. We need to think about the future. We envisage how our life will change because of our baby. We wonder if our baby will be healthy, we wonder what sex it will be, we wonder if it will take after its mum or dad, we worry if we will be able to care for it properly. We invest a vast amount of thought and energy into our baby before it is even born.

Month after month the physical and mental work of preparation for the coming birth takes place. The pregnancy period allows us time to make adjustment to the coming change. This is particularly necessary if this is to be a first child and we have to make that change from not being a parent into becoming either a mother or a father for the very first time. Second and subsequent children in a family also need this time of preparation. Each pregnancy is unique. Each potential birth will change our life in a unique way.

Not all pregnancies are welcomed with uniform delight. Even much wanted and longed-for pregnancies can bring with them fears and doubts and morning sickness.

In the early days, unplanned pregnancies may necessitate the need to make important decisions in a short space of time.

As the pregnancy progresses knowledge of the coming baby becomes public. It is almost impossible to hide the fact that one is five months pregnant. A baby is a part of a larger family group however far one is from home. As the news spreads family members begin to work out the change this newcomer will make in their lives; perhaps they will become a grandparent or an aunty or uncle or brother or sister to the new baby. For the parents-to-be the practical implications become increasingly important; where is the baby going to sleep, what clothes and goods will it need; how will it affect the family income, when will the mother have to give up work?

Pregnant And Then Not Pregnant
If, for one reason or another, we lose a baby, and the powerful process of preparation for birth is interrupted by miscarriage or termination, then both our body and our mind will be deeply affected. It is as if, whilst driving as fast as we can in one direction, we were to be suddenly instructed to go into reverse. Of course such an abrupt turning isn't possible - the best one could do might be to try and slam on the brakes, but even then the momentum would still carry us forward for a while. After a termination, the mother's body needs time to adjust to not being pregnant; and everyone who was anticipating the coming birth will also need to adjust to the loss of the potential future which seemed so recently to lie ahead.

The Unrecognised Loss
The loss of a baby before it has been born may not be recognised as

an important loss by our friends and relatives. They are not able to see who it is that we have lost, or what it is that we are grieving for.

Part of that work of grief might include the need to go over and over the circumstances surrounding our loss. Whether or not the loss was as a result of a decision we made, or someone else made, or because of natural causes outside of our control, we may still need to examine and explore those reasons which led to our loss - even though there may not necessarily be any easy answers to the questions we raise. This work of grief is particularly hard if our loss is unrecognised and we have been left to grieve alone.

Abortion

If we have had to have an abortion, for whatever reason - our health or the health of the baby or the particular circumstances we found ourselves in at the time of our pregnancy - we may also have chosen to keep that pregnancy and the ending of it, a secret from our friends or family.

In this case, there may be no-one we can turn to when we feel low and distressed. No-one with whom we can share our fears and anxieties and no-one who will sit with us if we feel the need occasionally to go back over the reasons why we had to make that decision.

Even if those around us know of the abortion, they may feel that we have no right to feelings of grief because we have created our own loss. If they feel we have done the wrong thing in having the abortion, then we can expect precious little sympathy from them. Even if they feel we have done the right thing, we may still be encouraged to get on with life and stop worrying about the past. After all, we may be told, we can always have another child.

Inspite of the fact that we might know our decision to abort was the only option open to us, there may be times when we still think about the baby we might have had, and feel intensely sad that its potential life had to be ended. Some women find they have strong feelings around the time that the baby would have been born.

How we are treated at the time of our abortion will affect our ability to accept what has happened to us. Certainly, it can be helpful to have the opportunity to talk out thoughts and feelings with a counsellor both before and after an abortion. And, like all losses there may be times long after the event when we need to think about it once again and with those thoughts might come quite powerful and unexpected feelings.

Miscarriage

The word miscarriage covers a wide range of loss - from the very early 'disappointment', to the baby which suddenly dies in the womb having survived many months of seemingly normal pregnancy.

Most miscarriages, however, occur in the early months of pregnancy and family and friends may have hardly been aware of the pregnancy before receiving news that the baby has been lost. On hearing of the miscarriage, they may be sad for the bereaved couple and for themselves; especially if it was, say, a much-wanted grandchild that has been lost, but it is unlikely that they will appreciate the vast amount of hopes and dreams that may already have been invested by the parents-to-be in their coming child, or how empty and hollow their lives will feel now that these have been so abruptly brought to an end.

The further into the pregnancy the more attached the mother will become to the living baby inside her body; the larger will be her awareness of it as a unique being containing its own potential; and the greater will be her grief when it dies.

All too often, grieving young couples are offered comfort with the suggestion that they can always "try again". They may attempt to comfort each other with that very same statement. And, of course, in time they may well have a beautiful, healthy baby but that will lie far ahead in the future.   Now they are facing an unexpected and frightening loss.

Few who have not lost a much-wanted baby through miscarriage can appreciate the pain and deep distress that such a loss might create - the sense that one is a failure as a mother, the feeling that there must be something very wrong with a body that rejects a baby. Accompanying the distress and pain may also be the fear that we may never be able to have a child. This fear naturally becomes much greater if this is a second miscarriage or even a third.

Why did it die? It is important to know as much as possible why the miscarriage happened. If we know what went wrong this time then it is possible we will be able to prevent such a loss happening again. It is through knowledge that we begin to accept bereavement and learn to trust the world again.

Sometimes there simply is no clear answer to our question. A proportion of early pregnancies do seem to end spontaneously in miscarriage. This does not mean that a subsequent pregnancy will end in miscarriage or that we will ever miscarry a child again.

There may be a definite reason why the miscarriage occurred and, in the light of this new knowledge, actions can be taken that will help prevent subsequent miscarriages.

The child lost through a miscarriage may have carried all a parent's hopes for the future for several months but when it dies, there may be very little left to remember it by. No grave, no memorial and no photographs. Although it existed physically within its mother's body, apart from the physical effects its passing may have had on that body, it will leave behind it only memories.

The Miscarriage Association (based in West Yorkshire) produces a regular newsletter which contains valuable knowledge on the various causes of miscarriage. Through the organisation those who have suffered a miscarriage can contact one another. Some find that it helps to talk with others who have been through a similar experience.

THE DEATH OF A BABY: BORN TO DIE

Once the pregnancy is confirmed, ahead of the parents lies a clearly defined path and, at the end of that path is one single goal, the birth of their baby or babies if twins are expected. As a parent we will know to within a week or so, when our baby is due and the arrangements for that birth; whether it is planned to take place in the home or in a hospital. If certain tests have been done, we may also even know the sex of our baby.

As the final weeks approach, an increasing number of checks will be made on both mother and unborn child. For the mother particularly, the baby within her womb, and the excitement and fears for its coming birth dominate all other thoughts. For the majority of parents all this tension and great expectation culminates in the successful birth of their child. Sadly, for some, there is no such happy ending.

Stillbirth

Some babies are born dead. Others, perhaps because they are born prematurely or very ill, or due to exceptional medical complications will only live a few hours or days after their birth.

Perhaps the first thing parents want to know is why has this happened. If the doctors and midwife do not know it may help them to find out if there is a post-mortem examination of your baby. Even this may not produce a clear answer.

Once, not so long ago, stillborn babies were simply taken away from their mothers. Fortunately, the work of the organisation SANDS (Stillbirth and Neonatal Death Society - 28 Portland Place, London, W1N 3DE) has helped educate nurses, doctors and other professionals in the importance of dealing with such a major loss in a proper and caring way. Now, in most hospitals, both parents will have the opportunity of seeing and holding their dead child if they wish to do so. A photographer may be available to take a picture of the baby which can be kept by the parents although it may be some time before they can bear to look at it.

If your baby is stillborn you will have to register his or her birth. The registrar will give you a certificate for burial. It is now possible for funeral and cremation services to be held for these very little children. The fact that they were born dead, or lived such a short time, does not mean that they will not be grieved by their parents and other family members. Unfortunately, the pain and grief of such a death creates is sometimes underestimated, the assumption made that, as there was hardly time to get to know the child, the loss will therefore be greatly reduced - and the dead baby and the grief all forgotten as soon as a live child comes along.

Often a coming baby will carry with it the hopes and dreams of its parents or grandparents. Babies can become symbols for the future; perhaps a sign that the family is growing, maturing and developing. The knowledge of the coming child can unite quarrelling family members and prospective parenthood can provide a focus and a clear way forward for couples whose life had previously seemed to be without a definite purpose.

The accidental, unplanned-for and initially unwanted pregnancy will have involved the parents-to-be in a great deal of hard work and emotional soul searching as they struggle to make the adjustment from shock, through to an acceptance of the coming child. Perhaps sacrifices may have had to be made along the way; the goodwill of one's family or the loss of a much-wanted career. Then there is the baby conceived after a long period of infertility or the one that follows a series of miscarriages. How precious they are and how terrible the thought of their loss.

When a baby dies at birth or soon after, all the hopes and dreams they carried with them disappear and their loss has to be acknowledged along with the life that has ended.

Quite apart from what the coming baby may stand for, even before its birth it will have a character all of its own. That process of getting to know the baby has been taking place for many months. From a very early stage a mother, and often her partner too, will begin to build a personality for the developing foetus in her womb, endowing the unborn baby with a whole range of feelings and reactions - "It must be a boy it's got such a strong kick" - "She loves pop music" - "Compared to my last, it's a very good baby."

Now, after the birth and the death, the baby that the mother holds in her arms and studies so carefully, may not be alive but it is still very real indeed. It has its own sex, it has hair and fingers and features and character and perhaps also its own name.

If the birth has taken place in hospital then, even if she is in a room of her own, the mother is aware that all around her other women are giving birth to healthy babies. Like them, her body is still suffering the effects of the birth, she may be bleeding, her breasts are sore and producing milk but there is no baby to feed; no reward for all the labour she has suffered.

And she will return without her baby, to a home that only a short time ago was made ready for a very different homecoming.

For a long time everything associated with the baby will bring sadness and pain; the baby clothes he or she would have worn, the cot with its blankets and sheets.

Can you be a mother if you have no baby? Can you call yourself a father if your baby dies at birth? These difficult questions confront any parent who loses an only child whether that child dies after living ten years or only a single day. There may be no child now to care for and nurture but the experience of being a mother or a father has taken place and become part of one's history and will remain so for ever. A stillborn child often has a very special place in the hearts and minds of its mother and father; a place which can never be usurped by subsequent children.

Cot Death

The long months of pregnancy are successfully completed, culminating in the birth of a lovely healthy child. The baby settles down well and slowly the parents begin to relax a little. A routine of feeding and sleeping and play is gradually established. The whole household accustoms itself to living with a baby - in a remarkably short period it is hard to remember a time before the baby arrived.

Then, one day, the baby dies. Often there is no illness before the death to warn parents of what is coming. Usually, the baby will die in its sleep; and when its mother or father goes to wake it for its feed or bath, it is found to be dead. 20 such deaths take place in this country every day.

Such sudden and inexplicable deaths cause great shock and pain to the parents and everyone who knows and has grown to love the baby. There can be no chance at all to prepare for such a tragedy. In a matter of seconds life moves from normality into a nightmare. Because the death is so unexpected it will have to be investigated. The police will be informed as a matter of course and a post mortem will have to take place.

The burning question in the mother and father's mind at such a time is why did our baby die, and could we have prevented its death? It is possible that no single cause for the loss of these babies will ever be discovered. Sadly, in spite of our increased medical sophistication, there still seems no way we are able to prevent the ending of these very young lives.

As parents we feel responsible for the lives of our babies. Even if there was absolutely no way in which we could have prevented the ending of that young life, everything in us will go on questioning our part in the death.

Suppose we had come home earlier? Could we have prevented it if we had done this instead of that? The fact that we know that we could not have prevented it, the fact that our doctor and the hospital and the inquest have all confirmed that we are in no way responsible for the death, does not mean that we will acquit ourselves. To question the events surrounding a death is part of that intensely painful early work of grief. Only when it is completed will we then be able to move forward into the future once again.

Many mothers who lose a baby describe themselves as feeling empty. There is nothing now for them to hold; a huge hole has opened up in the centre of their life where once there was a child. If there are other children in the family then they will still need to be cared for, but it can be hard to find the strength and energy to carry on caring for others at such a time.

The father of the baby may find that he has very confused feelings. He may feel that his first duty is to support his wife in her grief, that as a man he should remain in control of himself and his feelings. After all, there are arrangements to be made, the business of death takes time and a clear mind.

Sometimes employers are not as sympathetic as they could be and it may be hard to take time off work. Some men feel that it's preferable to be at work where at least they can relax and temporarily forget what has happened than in a home which is so full of pain and memories.

No two people will grieve at the same pace. When one needs to talk, the other might prefer silence. When one is feeling just a little optimistic the other might be at their lowest point.

The Foundation for the Study of Infant Deaths - 35 Belgrave Square, London, SW1X 8PS is an organisation which finances research into cot deaths, and also puts parents bereaved in this way in touch with one another. They operate a 24 hour helpline offering support and information to those who have suffered a cot death and their relatives.

A DEATH OUTSIDE THE FAMILY

Not all the people we love and care about are contained in our family groups. During our late teens and twenties we are likely to know quite a few people whose lives are involved closely with our own in one way or another. There will be our boyfriends and girlfriends, our lovers and our ex-lovers, the people we may share a house or flat with, our colleagues at work, or at college - all those people who have shared a common interest with us.

It may not be until we lose such a person that we become fully aware of the importance they had in our life. When they die, we may find ourselves viewing both ourselves and the world around us quite differently. Each loss will have its own special significance for us. It will create a reaction that is as unique and as personal as the relationship which has been ended by the death.

The death of a teacher may affect us deeply; not only because it may be the first time we confront death and bereavement, but because it may also interrupt our studies and our confidence in our ability to pass an exam. This loss of a teacher will also affect others in our class, and we may have to find a way of coping with their very different reactions alongside our own confused feelings (it isn't easy to face the fact that we are thoroughly fed-up that our personal plans are upset because someone has died).

The loss of our boss at work may suddenly threaten our position in the firm. The loss of a lover we knew years ago may turn our thoughts back to that long-distant past, and we may find ourselves grieving its loss as well as for the person who has died.

The death of someone we felt could have become a very important part of our life leaves us confused, and feeling as it we have been robbed of an opportunity to go forward.

Each death we face will steal part of our past, present or future, from us.

THE DEATH OF A FRIEND

Most of us recognise that we need at least one good friend if we are to live a reasonably happy life.

A friend is someone we can share our thoughts and feelings with. It is someone who likes us for what we are; someone that we can like in return.

Friendship is a relationship based on equality, although a good friendship will survive all manner of temporary inequalities, ups and downs, separations and changes of fortune.

Friendship is a word we reserve for special relationships. Our colleagues at work, or college, are not necessarily our friends. Although we may like them, and they us, at the end of the working day, we may not choose to spend our evenings in their company. We do choose to spend time with our friends, and friendship is built on the principle of choice. We may not choose our family or relatives, but we do choose our friends.

It is this special relationship which vanishes when a friend dies.

Changing Friends

Most of us have several different groups of friends. There will be our neighbourhood friends; friends we have known since we went to the same primary school. Then there are our secondary-school friends; and, later still, we may acquire friends from college, and our place of work. Out of each friendship-group we may keep in touch with only one or two special people.

Best Friends

From amongst our friends, most of us will have one particular person we call our best friend. Some people have the same best friend for years, others have a series of changing best friends, or a group of best friends - people they know they can always call up when they are fed up or lonely.

Best friends are important. They care about us and they know things about us that others don't because they are close to us. If we have known them a long time, then they carry a part of our history with them; they remember what we were like in the past, they can see the changes that have happened to us.

To lose such a friend is to lose a part of ourselves.

Changing Needs

Friendships need to be tough if they are to survive the wear and tear upon them. We do not always need our friends in the same way. When we are in the process of looking for a lover, then it is a great help to have friends to talk over the ups and downs, the successes and failures, of our search. When we find that one special person, then our friends often have to take a back seat in our lives for a while as we concentrate on developing our new relationship.

Once we have established a reasonably secure partnership, then we can turn back to our friends and include them in our lives once again. If they are now also in couple relationships this makes the basis of foursomes and a new friendship-group is formed.

Because friendships change over a period of time, it's easy to underestimate their importance. We may assume that, were they to end through separation or even death, our lives would not be seriously affected by their loss. It may not be until we lose a close friend that we become aware their going has opened up a huge hole within our life.

Loneliness and New Friends

Life without a best friend can be very hard indeed. Not to have that friend as part of our life can make us feel intensely lonely; no-one to share our thoughts with, no-one who will laugh in that special way, or cry with us when we get upset.

There may be no-one to go down to the pub with in the evening, or to the cinema, or theatre, or match.

Our best friend would probably have been the person who would have best understood our present sadness. Who would have been there at our side helping us through this difficult time.

It is through such close and caring relationships that we learn the art and skills of friendship. Once we have that important knowledge we will find a way of creating new friendships.

A special friend we have lost through death will remain in our thoughts and minds, but, eventually, we will go on to make new friends, and we will learn to laugh and share our thoughts and feelings with them.

HOW DID THEY DIE?

When we hear of the death of someone known to us, either personally or through the media, one of our first reactions is to ask, "How did they die - what was the cause of their death?"

The laws of this country pose the same questions. The moment a death occurs, a chain of events is set in motion which ensures that the circumstances surrounding the death are fully investigated. How somebody dies is important. It is not enough to declare someone dead. The rites of passage, the funeral or cremation will not be allowed to take place until the first stages of that investigation have been completed.

Society as a whole also reflects this need to know how and why death happens. Few newspaper articles relating the news of a celebrity's death will not include either the cause of death, if it is known, or the possible cause, if it is still in doubt.

Some kinds of death are so dramatic that they make the newspaper headlines. They fascinate and interest us even if the people whose lives have ended are completely unknown to us. Suicide, murder, disaster and war deaths all fall into this category.

We do not have the same fascination in the process of birth. When hearing of a new baby few of us wish to know how it was born. There is, of course, less variety in the act of birth - it is possible that our greater interest in death lies in the fact that it still lies ahead for us.

Death may be a taboo subject, but we are fascinated by it and take every opportunity to explore the ending of people's lives. We watch death on the news and in films and videos. We read about it in books and newspapers. In doing so, we are confronting our own potential death. We try each life-ending on as if it were a new suit of clothes. We explore what we would feel like if it were ourselves. After all, it might have been us in that road accident, or in the plane which crashed. It could have been our father or wife in that terrible fire, or it just might be our child who was murdered.

When the worst happens and death comes to us - when it is our father or our wife or our child that dies - then we will question and explore it all in a very different way. This time it is personal. This is our loss, our shock, our life that has been shattered. This time we expect to find the right answers to those important questions.

Part of the early, painful work of grief involves investigation into the events leading up to, and surrounding the death. In our search for understanding of that ending, we will need to go over and over the past; examining it for clues, reliving the sequence of happenings that led towards the death. Different endings will create a different effect upon us. The death which follows a long terminal illness may still shock us when it comes, but it will not have the same impact upon us as the death which strikes with no warning at all.

Some deaths are better than others. If someone we love dies with dignity it can help us in our grief. An example of great courage can give *us* the courage we need to go on in the bleak early days of our bereavement. The opportunity to share with a dying person their hopes and fears can enable us to explore our own future loss, and may also ease the practical problems of bereavement. Being able to say "Thank you", or "You mattered to me", or, "I love you", or even just "Goodbye", is so important.

Some deaths are worse than others. The undignified, painful death of someone we love leaves us with bitter painful memories. The death which could have been prevented makes us long to turn back the clock and set in motion those events that could and should have prevented it. The death which follows incompetence or neglect by those who were in charge of the situation leaves us angry and wondering how far we should take up the fight on behalf of the ones we have lost. The sudden death allows no goodbyes, no parting words. The violent death leaves us with violent thoughts.

Good or bad, we will need to explore the circumstances surrounding the death of the person we have lost very carefully indeed. The more distressing the nature of the death, the harder that work of exploration will be.

UNNATURAL DEATH

Deaths which result from criminal acts such as murder or manslaughter, or from suicide, disasters or war can all be classified as violent deaths. Few are foreseen or anticipated, and many happen with no warning at all. Quite suddenly, where once there was a living person, there is now no-one. Such deaths create great shock.

Unfinished Business

The sudden death leaves behind it so much unfinished business. There has been no time to make amends if there have been quarrels. No time for wills, or funeral plans. No time for straightening out financial matters. No time to tell the person we have lost how much they meant to us and how much we will miss them when they are gone. No time to say thank you. No time even, to say goodbye.

Bad Memories

The actual manner of the death may leave behind it memories or mental pictures that are deeply distressing to recall.

The work of grief in the early months of bereavement involves the need to replay the events surrounding the death over and over again in one's mind. The more distressing those events were, the more painful is this process of recall.

If we had been a part of the accident or disaster that caused the death, we may find ourselves suffering from nightmares and disturbed sleep patterns for many months afterwards. If we were injured in the accident, we will be coping with the loss of health and lack of freedom of movement alongside our loss of the one that we love.

If we were many miles away when the death came, then the pictures we have of what happened that day will come from other people who were there, or from the media, or from the inquest. If we don't have any information about how the death happened, we may create, in our imagination, a picture far worse than any reality. If we were not present at the death, but saw the body a little later on - we may retain pictures of damage and injury.

Violent death creates violent memories which lodge in our minds for ever. The effect of them will be greatest in the early months of our bereavement but they will continue to have some influence upon us for the rest of our life.

Unlike a computer, our brain does nοτ ʜave a DELETE, CLEAR or WIPE program when information which we find deeply disturbing is fed into it.

We have to find a way of living on alongside such memories, and accept that we are changed forever because of the dramatic events which have taken place in our history. We have become someone who has experienced the violent death of someone they love. We have no choice over that definition, but eventually we do have a choice as to whether or not it becomes our 'main claim to fame' - whether we allow that event to control and dominate our life for ever - or eventually progress to being defined in other ways.

Too Painful To Speak About

It can be hard to find a way of talking about very painful events, and, if we do have a need to, we may find that people around us soon stop listening to our story; perhaps because they find it painful to hear, or because they feel it is bad for us to dwell on such things and they want to encourage us to forget.

Although it is really impossible to put such important and emotional events to one side at will, to our surprise, we may find that there are times when we do forget. Times when the business of life goes on much as normal. But, every so often, the need to remember comes back, and with it the need, once again, to talk about what has happened. The more violent the death the harder it can be for those around us to know how to help us or what to say.

Having an outside source of support can help at such times. Someone trained to listen who will not be over-burdened by our pain and sadness. Someone not our friend, but someone able to take the strain of our grief and thereby release our friends to be just that - our friends.

No Body No Grave

In some cases there may be no body to bury or cremate. It is hard to accept a death as reality if there is no tangible evidence that it has happened - no real ending to that life. The natural stage of searching-on for that person we know who has died is extended when we are given no absolute proof of death.

It is not simply that *we* require proof; practically, insurance companies may be reluctant to pay out without evidence of the death, and rights to pension benefits, or the like, may be withheld for similar reasons. For a while, we may find ourselves existing in a kind of 'limbo world'; suspended between being bereaved and not being bereaved.

Police Inquests And Coroners

Violent deaths will involve investigation by the police, and an inquest to determine the cause of the death. There may also be a trial if the death is the result of a criminal action. Suddenly, we could find ourselves in a vastly different world from the one we were safely part of only a short time ago.

Public Death/The Media

Such deaths attract publicity and disturb the natural pattern of public burial, and, of course, the right to grieve privately for our own private loss. We may find ourselves the centre of attention from local (or even national) journalists. Violent death is news, and reports of it may appear several times over in the newspapers or perhaps on television.

How we may wish to deal with reporters will depend very much on our particular circumstances. Sometimes the media can play an important investigative role which helps us in our personal need for information. We may also feel that, by telling our story, we will ensure that others are protected from having to go through a similar loss. In this way some good at least comes from our tragedy.

If we do decide to talk with journalists we may need some protection ourself. Be careful over the telephone! What we may feel is a purely sympathetic conversation may well be taken down in note form as we speak and we may find our words quoted in tomorrow's paper. If we are aware that we will be quoted ask the journalist to give a precis of what they will be saying. If the article is to appear in a magazine ask to see it before it appears and for the right to change any inaccuracies; similarly with television interviews which will be broadcast at a later date.

If we do not wish to talk, then a simple statement that we are too upset to speak to anyone is usually all that is necessary. If we need to rest but find it hard to do so because of interruptions by telephone or visitors, then we need a good friend to guard us for a while.

Our story may be newsworthy when the event actually happens, also at the time of the investigation or inquest and at any subsequent event which ties in with our particular loss. At each point we have a choice as to whether or not we may wish to speak with any journalists that approach us.

Violent Death/Violent Grief

Violent deaths create a violent response in those who are bereaved by them. There may be great anger against the person or institution seen to be to blame for the death. There may be frustration if there is no just punishment. There can be extreme guilt if it is felt that, with the appropriate action or words, we could have prevented the death from happening.

Murder

The knowledge that someone we love has been murdered may come with no warning at all. We pick up a telephone or answer the door and, in a moment, our life is totally changed. Alternatively, there may be a period when the threat of death and murder hangs over us for days or even weeks. Someone we love has gone missing; there is cause for great concern; the police are investigating the disappearance; a search is in operation. The days are filled with endless questions from the investigators, journalists and friends, and we are torn between hope and dread. Until the day comes when the hope is finally ended.

If someone we love has been murdered, we may have to live for ever with the knowledge that the last moments of their life contained fear, panic, or pain. They will only have suffered those events once, but we may relive them time and time again in our minds.

When we love someone we want to keep them safe from harm. We are not always able to do this. Great harm has happened and in the early months of our bereavement we may find ourselves searching and re-searching the past in a desperate and futile attempt to undo the events that led up to the death. If only she had not gone that evening, or we had used the car, or he had come home the other way, or stayed the night.

What we are still searching for at this time is a different ending because we simply cannot accept or bear this brutal ending of life that has been forced upon us and the one we love.

Because we loved the person who has died, we take a personal interest in their death; we long for their murderer to be captured - and if they are, we long for them to pay a just punishment for the crime they have committed.

It is almost impossible to stay apart from this intense involvement with the aftermath of such a death.

This search for just retribution is only one part of the work of grief which we need to do if we are ever to learn to live our lives fully once again. It is important that we should allow ourselves space away from the anger and bitterness from time to time, both for our own sake and for the sake of those we live with and who still need us.

How a life is ended should not become more important than the life that was lived so fully right up until that end. The one we have lost is not just a murder victim and we need to remember and talk about them with love and humour as well as sadness and pain. The ultimate loss lies in not having them here with us now. This is the loss we should face however they may have died. Alongside that loss lies the additional burden of the very particular circumstances surrounding their death, the fact that they were murdered.

Suicide

Technically, suicide is described as violent death - although undoubtedly some suicides are more violent than others.

A death by suicide can leave all who are bereaved by it confused and experiencing deeply disturbing and difficult emotional responses. So often there is the feeling that such a death - more than any other - should, and could, have been prevented.

There is a great need to investigate the events leading up to it and to try to find out why someone should have chosen to take the actions they did to end their own life.

Such investigation is bound to involve a degree of guilt or anger. The 'if onlys' can be endless - If only the clock could be put back, and life relived in a slightly different way! - If only the doctor had acted more promptly! - If only I had stayed with them! If only the death had been prevented.

Why Suicide?

Some suicides come at the end of a period of deep depression and mental anguish. The fact of death is shocking, but often not perhaps totally unexpected. It is not easy to live alongside someone who is suffering from a deep and long-lasting depression - and the grief following such an ending will be different from the grief experienced after a suicide which comes seemingly out of the blue. There may even be a sense of relief that, at long last, their unhappiness and suffering is over.

There are many different kinds of suicide: from the almost accidental, to the minutely planned act. By killing him or herself, a person may be saying, "I cannot bear the pain of living on any more." Or they may be making a more specific statement; "You have hurt me." Or "I have failed you."

It is impossible for those of us left behind not to respond. We may feel guilty at having failed them, or hurt by their rejection of us. Or angry - How dare they do this to us? What have we done to deserve such pain and humiliation?

Sometimes suicide notes are left behind which offer up some explanation for the reasons behind the death. However, these also reflect the often confused feelings of the person planning to take their own life and should be taken and understood in that context. Sometimes a suicide death remains a mystery. We, who are left behind, need to search for understanding but there may be no answers.

The vast majority of people who lose a job or a partner or who go bankrupt will not try to kill themselves. Those that do are often vulnerable for many different reasons and a life event, normally quite bearable, seems to them, at that particular moment in time, to be unbearable.

Not so long ago it was a criminal offence to attempt to take one's own life and suicide was also seen as a crime against God. This placed a heavy burden on those bereaved by suicide. Fortunately this stigma no longer exists and the friends and relatives of those that take their own life are now free to talk openly about their loss and the particular pain that such an ending brings to those who are left behind.

In the deep sadness and depression that follows such a loss we may come closer to understanding their wish to end their life as we struggle to make sense of our own. If we find ourselves thinking of our own death then it is important that we find help for ourselves as soon as possible; that we tell our doctor how we are feeling and ask for the support we need from professionals, friends and family. At such a difficult period in our life, we deserve the best available support and should make sure that we get it!

Death Through Disaster
In a disaster, a number of people are killed or seriously injured as a result of the same incident. Disasters strike without warning. Suddenly the plane crashes to the ground, the boat begins to sink, the volcano erupts, the fire ignites or the gunman starts to shoot. Where once, only seconds ago, there was order and security, now there is fear, panic and perhaps great courage as people struggle to survive personally and to help those around them.

These catastrophic events can produce extensive trauma for all those who live through them. This is known as post-traumatic shock and symptoms can include uncontrollable bouts of shaking, frequent nightmares, sleeplessness, inability to concentrate, difficulty in breathing and sudden deeply disturbing mental flashbacks to the disaster.

These can still be occurring many months after the event. Policemen, ambulance drivers and anyone who becomes involved with a disaster can be deeply affected by it for a long time.

Survivors may feel guilt because they managed to survive whilst those around them died or because their injuries were less severe. Those survivors who lose close friends or relatives in the disaster will be coping simultaneously with two major crises; the personal experience they have lived through plus their grief at the loss they have suffered.

There is no way that society can every be fully prepared for a disaster. However efficiently the community responds, in the ensuing confusion, family and friends of the victims of a disaster may find it hard to get accurate information about their loved ones. They may have to make rapid decisions about whether or not they should view the body. If they are advised against doing so, then they may regret this later on.

Increasingly, those involved in and bereaved by a disaster are finding a way to join up with one another and share information and sources of support. This is important because disaster victims can be under unique pressure. Like other bereaved people they want to know how and why the disaster occurred. However, it may take months, or even years, for a disaster to be fully investigated; determining liability - which may also involve large scale financial damages - has to be done with great care.

Disaster victims may find themselves under other pressures in the days and weeks following the death. Offers of help of one kind or another may pour in, confusing the bereaved family who, at that time may still be deeply shocked. This is not to underestimate the value of having someone there to listen when we need to talk. Someone who will understand our need to know all the facts, however unpleasant. Someone who will not be frightened by our grief, someone who recognises our need to go back repeatedly to those terrifying moments when, for us, life was changed for ever.

Understandably, disasters attract a great deal of publicity. A disaster situation poses a threat to everyone - people sitting in their front rooms watching television or reading the headlines in the paper will be saying to themselves - that could have been me or my child or my partner, my parent or my best friend. It is often through persistent press agitation that improvements are made which prevent future disasters. However, those bereaved through such a major event can find the attention from television and newspaper reporters intrusive and disturbing at times. Their private grief becomes a symbol for the nation's sadness but unfortunately they can not turn off the effects of their loss with the switch on the television set or put it to one side like yesterday's newspaper.

War

War creates two different kinds of casualties. There are those who are called 'the innocent victims' - men, women and children caught up in events beyond their control, who are killed, maimed or bereaved in a war situation. For such people war is a series of disasters and they will be subject to all the trauma and stress of those living through, or being bereaved by, a major disaster.

Then there are those who are actively engaged in the war, the soldiers who fight for their country. Men (and women) who are trained for just such a situation and who go into the war zone with the knowledge that, in doing so they are putting their lives in danger. These are most likely to be quite young men who, if they die, will leave behind them grieving parents or young widows with young children.

Those who lose loved ones in the armed forces face their own special kind of loss and grief. There is some preparation for bereavement because the risk is acknowledged. There is also often an acceptance of why that risk is being taken. A job needs to be done and these particular men have the courage and training necessary to do that job. At a time of war the men who fight on their country's behalf are deeply respected.

However, there is all the difference in the world between thinking about the possibility of losing someone and that loss actually taking place. The death of a healthy young person is so intensely hard to accept even if we feel we understand the reason for that death.

The families of those fighting in a war face long periods of uncertainty. "Is my son (or husband or brother) still safe?" As long as loved ones remain in the battle zone they are in danger and the tension continues.

In war, there is not always a clear ending to life and some men are stated as 'missing in action' for a long time; their relatives not knowing whether or not their loved ones are dead or alive. If death does come it may be instantaneous or happen after months of struggling for survival against the effects of serious injury.

It is not always possible to get information about the events surrounding the death. The authorities may not know what happened or, for security reasons, be unable to say what happened or they may even feel they have a duty to protect relatives from the pain of the truth. Although well meaning, such protection rarely works. Eventually the truth usually emerges one way or another. The majority of bereaved people express the wish to know that truth however hard it may be to bear the knowledge it contains.

SSAFA - the Soldiers' Sailors' And Airman's Families Association and local Family Service Units provide valuable practical and emotional support for those who lose someone whilst fighting for their country. Families living on the bases support one another at times of crisis. However, if a husband is killed or seriously wounded, at some point his family will have to vacate their accommodation on the base. Wives and children will have to leave behind them those who most understand their loss; best friends, teachers, neighbours, their doctor. It is very hard indeed to have to start a new life in new surroundings at a time when one is most vulnerable.

Those who die in battle are often idealised. Wives and parents may find it hard to find a place to express all the negative and 'bad' feelings which are nearly always somewhere beneath the surface in the months and years following such a great loss. They may feel obliged to appear brave and in control of themselves when sometimes they just want to scream out their pain and anger and frustration, that sense of - Why me? Why my husband? Why my son?

Children who have lost a father or older brother in the war may also feel under pressure to live up to the high standards set by the deceased. It is important to hold on to the fact that brave men also have feelings of fear. It is good to see an increasing number of 'fighting' men prepared to talk openly about their feelings and even cry in public.

For the bereaved, finding a safe place to scream or just be ourselves is important. Counsellors, ministers, support groups and friends and family can all play a part in giving us the backing we need at this intensely sad and painful time.

Army wives can be used to long periods apart from their husbands. Such separations can make us more capable of living on our own but it may also mean that it will take that much longer for the death to be fully realised. Long after the funeral and the memorial service has passed, a small part of us, may still be waiting for the key to turn in the door and for everything to be alright again. Wars end. The loss we have suffered goes on. We will learn to live again but life can never be the same again.

Accidental Death

The inquest brings in a verdict of accidental death or death by misadventure. This means that a decision has been made that no-one is legally to blame for what has happened and no criminal charges will be brought in connection with the death.

Each year many people in this country die as a result of an accident. This may have taken place in the home, in the street, in a car, at school or in our back garden. Motor bikes crash, we fall off ladders, and tumble into rivers. However carefully we seek to protect ourselves or those we love, accidents do still happen. By definition, accidents are unplanned and unexpected. There is little we can do to prevent them happening.

In retrospect we will look back and try to undo the particular set of circumstances that combined to create the accident that killed the person we love. We may curse ourselves for failing to see the consequences of that particular action or curse other people for what they did or failed to do. But ultimately we are drawn back to that word - accident. How insignificant it seems when compared to the loss we have suffered and the pain we are feeling now. How can something accidental deprive us and the one who has died of so much?

Sadly, the young are more likely to die as a result of accident than the middle-aged or elderly. The young are active and on the move. They are great experimenters in life, and often it is the bravest and most courageous that expose themselves to the greatest risk of damage.

Like other unnatural deaths, those caused by accident are unprepared for, sudden, shocking and deeply distressing. It takes a very long time to understand and begin to accept the consequences of such a loss.

DEATH THROUGH NATURAL CAUSES

The majority of people in this country die as a result of natural causes. Although disasters and murders may dominate the headlines they have little statistical significance. Over 90% of all the deaths taking place in this country occur to those over sixty years of age; and the vast majority of these deaths will be due to either heart disease or cancer. The heart attack may strike suddenly, destroying life in a matter of seconds, whilst the patient with terminal cancer may require a long period of nursing care either in hospital or at home. The reverse is also possible; the heart attack may leave someone alive but an invalid, and cancer is capable of taking life within a very short time of the diagnosis.

Slow or swift, unlike the violent death, nothing from outside has led directly to the death; it has been caused simply by something failing to function properly within the body of the deceased.

Sudden Death
The heart attack is the most common form of sudden natural death, although there are other conditions that can also cause an abrupt and unexpected ending to a life.

How can someone be alive and well one moment in time, and dead the next? How can we possibly accept such a vast change? How can we live in a world which is capable of throwing such changes at us? How can we trust life again?

The sudden death leaves us confused and deeply shocked. We may be in a state of shock for the first hours of our bereavement; feeling sick, our skin clammy, our breathing irregular, and our temperature lowered. Even when this state passes, the shock remains as a kind of numbness - creating a sense of unreality and distance from the world around us. Such shock can act as a defence against the pain of reality, and it may enable us to complete the business of death, helping us deal with the funeral director, doctor and solicitor. Many people looking back to this time say that they have little memory of it, or say they remember feeling like a robot, completing the various tasks almost automatically. The experience of such feelings are not unique to those who lose someone with little or no warning, but they are likely to be intensified and exaggerated in such situations.

The Diagnosis

"I am afraid that the tumour is malignant." There can be no good way of breaking such bad news. There comes a point when our secret suspicions become fact, when we learn that we, or someone we love, has a certain kind of cancer or Aids or any one of the many illnesses which threaten life. The very names of such illnesses seem frightening and, in the beginning, it can be hard to say the word to ourself let alone to other people. Some illnesses, such as Aids, carry with them additional fears and problems.

The more information we have about our particular illness and the particular effects it is having on us (or our loved one) the more we will feel in control of our situation. Many people suffering from life-threatening diseases become experts on that subject and understandably so. Most of the major sicknesses have their own organisation offering information and support for those suffering from it and their relatives.

Almost Sudden Death

Some illnesses strike fast and hard; moving in a matter of days or weeks from the first symptoms through to the need for tests, hospitalisation, diagnosis, and then, unavoidably, death.

Such rapid progress from health, to sickness, to death may give very little time for preparation for the coming ending. And we do need time to take in the fact that the illness is serious; that it might even be life threatening; that hope is very insecure; that death is a real possibility; that death is the only likely outcome.

The sudden onset of a serious illness or critical health condition places us in a nightmare situation from which, at a later date, we expect to wake and take up our normal life once again. By nature we are optimists; we tend to look for the best outcome; we do not expect those we love to die with very little warning. When they do, when we wake to find that the nightmare is a reality, then we are shocked and distressed and confused.

Terminal Illness

Some illnesses last months or even years; with plenty of time to face the possibility of death; to make that will, and attempt to tie up the many little loose ends of life - too much time perhaps. We learn to live with the fact of serious illness, and even cease to see it as a real threat. We believe the recovery which happened previously will happen again - until one day, the miracles end, and we find ourselves deeply shocked, even though the illness has been serious and long term.

Nursing Care

Illness often necessitates the need for intensive nursing care, either at home, in hospital, or a hospice. This will mean altering the routine of the home as everyone struggles to adapt to the changing needs of the patient.

Patients who have an operation or a short-term serious illness may find that they have almost too many visitors around their bedside. The patient who is ill for a long period of time may find it far harder to maintain contact with the outside world. A great many people are uncomfortable in the hospital or sick room situation; they don't know what to say to an ill person, and the regular visiting or care of the patient may be left to just one or two close relatives and friends. These carers may find that their lives become increasingly bound up in caring for the patient's needs - which can be considerable at such a time. Caught up in the world of illness, hospitalisation, visiting, medical care and drugs, the gap between the carers themselves, and their friends and relatives tends to increase as the time passes.

When the patient eventually dies, we lose not just someone we love very much indeed, but also the whole focus of our life. Suddenly there is no-one to care for. The battle for life which has been waged for so long has been lost. Others may see the death only as a welcome release and not be able to understand that, for the carer, it can also mean the loss of everything which gave life its purpose.

Pain And Discomfort

Inspite of advancements in medical knowledge, some people do experience considerable pain and discomfort in the last stages of a terminal illness.

If we love someone, everything inside us wishes to protect them from such pain; but, sadly, we may not be able to do so. All we can do is stand by them when they need us most.

After the death, we cannot wipe the images of their pain and sickness from our memories. They may be especially vivid in the early months of our loss, and emerge once again as we reach the anniversary of those painful events.

There can be some comfort gained from knowing that everyone did their very best to ease the pain. If, however, we have criticisms of the care the deceased received, then, as soon as we can, we may need to formalise them into a specific complaint against a particular person or authority.

We may also find that we have complaints against ourselves for not being there when needed - for failing to find the courage necessary to stay with them in their pain. It is hard to watch someone struggling to live on, against all odds. There will be times when we feel overwhelmed by everything; when we are exhausted and tired, when we need to be normal again, just for one day - or even an hour.

If the deceased was brave, then their courage may have enabled us to cope. It may not be until their death that the full impact of loss and loneliness begins to strike home.

Keeping Secrets

In an attempt to protect other members of the family, the full seriousness of the illness may be kept a secret. Sometimes patients themselves are not told, perhaps because it is felt that this would deprive them of hope - and without hope they would collapse into depression.

Many people feel that to admit that they could die is to make themselves vulnerable to death. This is, or course, hocus-pocus. It is possible to face the fact that we have not got long to live and, at the same time, hold onto the hope that the time we have left will be a useful and good time.

Sometimes the patient is aware of the diagnosis, but chooses to protect their family from the knowledge. Sometimes a collusion of silence exists, with all family members knowing the situation but feeling it best not to speak of it to the others. Such silence requires great restraint. It means putting our own needs to one side for the benefit of the one most vulnerable.

Within those families that are not able to share the fact of the coming ending with one another there is considerable loss - the loss of precious energy needed in the pretence that all will be alright in the end, and the loss of the opportunity to make final statements; to settle one's affairs and finish off the business of a lifetime.

In a family which is not openly confronting the possibility of death, all the members are prevented from expressing their true feelings and making a proper ending with the dying person. When the death happens there may be a sense of lost opportunity and unfinished business and this will become part of the work of early grief.

Life Goes On

Such large life happenings do not fit easily into late adolescence or young adulthood; a time when there is a need to be looking outward from the family or concentrating inwards on that personal struggle for the creation of the new adult self. This demands much energy and concentration; it is not easy to put such work to one side and become involved in the drama of someone else's illness and death. A drama where often all the main parts have been taken and one can only stand on the sidelines feeling helpless and bewildered.

How the death happened is of great importance in the early weeks and months of bereavement; for it is then that we need to investigate and try and make sense of the events surrounding our loss.

HELP!

We have investigated our personal history which will have affected those internal resources we will need to draw upon when confronting a loss. We have looked at who it was we have lost and the effect that loss will have on our life. We have considered how the death happened and the special circumstances attached to that unique ending of a life. The fourth and final influence over how we will grieve will be the amount of help and support available to us at the time of death and during our bereavement.

All too often we are expected to undertake the shattering and distressing effect of being bereaved with virtually no support at all. We may find ourselves deep in unknown territory, not knowing how we should be thinking, feeling or acting. So, what kind of help might we need, and where are we most likely to find it?

What Does Not Help

Perhaps it is easier to begin by defining what is generally not helpful at such a time.

It isn't helpful to be told we will get over it in time.

It isn't helpful to be told to pull oneself together.

It isn't helpful to be told that things could be worse.

It isn't helpful to be told it's all for the best.

It isn't helpful to be told that we must now support someone else.

It isn't helpful to be told that it's all God's Will.

It isn't helpful to be told about someone else's bereavement.

It isn't helpful to be ignored by friends and not asked out.

It isn't helpful for people to pretend that nothing has happened.

What Does Help

It does help knowing people care about us.

It does help having someone to listen to us when we want to talk.

It does help knowing we don't have to talk if we don't want to.

It does help to learn about grief and bereavement.

The Death of the Person Who Helps Us

It may be that the person we have lost is the very one who has always been there to give us support and understanding. We will need to look for another source of help if this is so.

Who Can Help Us?

All too often a death which affects us will also be affecting those we would expect to be our main source of help and support. Involved with their own sadness, they may find it impossible to reach out and console us in ours. If this is so, we will need to find an alternative source of support for a while.

Being There

Support at its simplest level means someone who is prepared to stay with us and work with us at our own pace - someone who accepts that we will be deeply affected by the death, but understands that we may still have other needs outside those of our grief, someone who will listen when we need a listener. Such a person could be our closest friend, our mother or father, a relative, a neighbour, a priest or minister, a teacher, or counsellor.

Alternative Help

A wide range of professional and non-professional people are out there ready to help us. The only problem is how to make contact. They don't know we need their help until we let them know we exist.

WITH A LITTLE HELP FROM MY FRIENDS

Having good friends can be so important when we are struggling through the bewildering and ever-changing emotional landscape of grief.

Never more than now do we need a secure background; somewhere to escape to where the atmosphere is not totally clouded by grief, somewhere where normal things continue to happen to normal people. A place where we are accepted more for who we are than for what has happened to us - however traumatic and distressing that happening may have been. A place where we know that our bereavement can be openly acknowledged if necessary, where we and our feelings are accepted.

Sadly, friends do not always seem able to supply the necessary security and care needed after a major loss. For every grieving person who describes the support they have received from their friends as "wonderful", there is another who feels confused and let down by friends who seem unwilling or unable to offer them anything, even friendship.

The sense of betrayal when friends fail us can be enormous.

Surely that's what friends are for, to stand by us when we need them most! How could they do this to us?

Not Knowing How to Help

So often friends simply don't know how to help us. They worry that they might say or do the wrong thing and upset us. After all, this is a totally new situation for them and they are not at all sure of the rules.

Would we want to be invited to a party a few days after the death? They don't know the answer. If they invite us, we might think them insensitive, and yet if they don't, maybe we will think they have excluded or forgotten us.

As we, the bereaved person have only a very hazy idea of what we want in the early weeks of bereavement it is hardly surprising that our friends are equally at a loss. We are new at being bereaved and they are new at having a bereaved friend. There are bound to be mistakes and misunderstandings.

They invite us to the party and we can't bear the laughter and leave early and they are left feeling guilty. They don't invite us and we feel excluded and hurt and they feel guilty at hurting us. Such confusion rapidly leads to irritation on their part - "How am I to know what she wants!" And self pity on ours - "They don't want me anymore!"

There is only one way of finding out what a bereaved person feels like or wants to do, and that is to ask them. If we are bereaved then there is only one way to help our friends help us and that is by telling them what makes us feel better and what makes us feel more alone and more unhappy.

We have to be able to explain why we needed to leave the party early. We have to tell our friends that sometimes we can't talk at all and at other times we need to go on and on and on about our feelings and our fears and our hopes and our dreams. As we gradually learn ourselves so we can pass that knowledge on to our friends.

It is worth recognising that because of our bereavement we are not capable of being a very good friend to anyone for a while. Because we are dealing with such a large event in our life we have less ability to help our friends deal with all the hundred and one smaller events that are happening in theirs. Against the fact of death their problems with their partners or work anxieties may seem to us to be totally insignificant. We are living in a world shattered by the loss of one of the most important people in our life and we probably have very little patience with the fact that they are worried about their hair or have quarrelled with a neighbour.

Our sensitive friends will recognise this change in us and how we see the world but may still be unsure of how to help us. Should they continue to bring us their problems and stories on the grounds that it will help us relax and feel part of things again; or, should they keep all that side of their life away from us and concentrate purely on our needs? Would it be insensitive to mention their mother if it was a mother that we had lost? If a child, would it be better to leave the children at home? Should the dead person be mentioned by name or left out of the conversation?

There are no rules that cover all such situations; no absolute right or wrong way to behave. It takes courage to broach the subject of death with a bereaved person. It takes courage to ask - "Does it hurt if I talk about my mother?" "Would you rather I left the children at home or brought them with me?" "Do you mind me talking about him?"

A major bereavement will temporarily upset the balance of friendships and it takes patience and a willingness to listen and learn - on both sides - if friendships are to survive the onslaught of grief. However, the friends we do keep through these dark days are likely to be friends for life. They have become a part of our experience. Their lives too, will be changed.

Good-Time Friends

Not all of our friends will be able to help us when we are grieving. Some people simply cannot bear loss or the expression of deep emotions. They can still remain an important part of our lives. They will be the friends we turn to when we need to escape from our grief and hopefully they will go on being our friends when we have come through this black time of our life. Our long-term friends reflect our history. They will be able to remember us before our loss. They are able to compare the person we were then to the person we have become. This is very important; they identify us when we are in the process of searching for a new identity and are feeling lost and confused. Good-time friends can be kept on ice until we are ready to have a good time again.

Helping the Helpers

If possible it would be better if we had several sources of support and help around us. If we find ourselves leaning very heavily on one particular friend after our bereavement, it might be worth checking to see that our friend has somewhere they can offload their feelings. Someone who is supporting them just as they are supporting us. It is hard work being the friend of someone who is grieving.

However good our sources of support may be, there will be times when they must fail us. After a major bereavement there is really only one person we want - the one who has died. No-one can take away our feelings or can put themselves truly in our place and understand exactly what we are going through. Knowing that those around us at are trying to understand and willing to listen does help, just a little, to ease some of that sense of isolation and fear that death can bring with it.

HELP FROM OTHERS IN A SIMILAR SITUATION

It can help to talk with someone who has experienced a loss similar to our own and who can understand a little of what we are going through. Some bereaved people have established self-support organisations which enable those going through similar losses to get in touch with one another. They will also be able to provide special knowledge and understanding of the problems and emotions generated by particular kinds of loss. Such organisations will try and ensure that those who act as helpers have reached a point in their own loss where they are able to concentrate on the needs of the more newly bereaved person.

It can help just to know someone who has actually survived such a loss.

Like Us But Different

It helps to remember that no two losses are ever the same, and no two people will grieve in exactly the same way. Even if we find someone who has lost the same relationship as we have, we will rapidly discover the differences between their loss and our own. We may need to spend time with that person to search out the common ground which might eventually become the basis of a real friendship.

Research

We may have to research our local area to find out if there are any self-support organisations meeting nearby.

The national headquarters of the major charities dealing with different forms of bereavement will usually be able to put people in touch with individual members, or local groups.

British Pregnancy Advisory Service – Austy Manor, Wootton Wawen, Solihull B95 6BX Information line: 020 7612 0208 email: www.bpas.org – Offers various services including counselling for an unwanted pregnancy and post-abortion counselling.

CancerBACUP – 3 Bath Place, Rivington Street, London EC2A 3JR Freeline: 0808 800 1234 Information: 020 7613 2121 email: info@cancerbacup.org website: www.cancerbacup.org.uk – Offers information, support and counselling for anyone affected by cancer, or the death of someone from cancer.

Child Death Helpline – (no postal contact) Helpline: 0800 282 986 every evening 7pm-10pm, Mon, Wed, Fri, 10am-1pm – Offers support for anyone affected by the death of a child of any age. The helpline is staffed by bereaved parents.

The Compassionate Friends – 53 North Street, Bristol BS3 1EN Helpline: 0117 9539 639 Mon-Fri 10am-4pm then 5pm-10.30pm email: info@tcf.org.uk website: www.tcf.org.uk – An international organisation for bereaved parents. They also have groups for parents of murdered children and a 'shadow of suicide' group.

Cruse Bereavement Care – 126 Sheen Road, Richmond, Surrey TW9 1UR Tel: 020 8940 4818 Helpline: 0870 167 1677 email: info@crusebereavementcare.org.uk website: www.crusebereavementcare.org.uk - Offers counselling to all bereaved and runs some groups for the widowed, widowed parents and young bereaved people.

Foundation for the Study of Infant Deaths – 11-19 Artillery Row, London SWIP 1RT 24hr Helpline: 020 7233 2090 email: fsid@sids.org.uk website: www.sids.org.uk/fsid - have contacts throughout the country to help those bereaved by a cot death.

Samaritans – Telephone: 08457 909090 website: www.samaritans.org – 24hr confidential telephone service for people who are in despair and feel suicidal.

Sands (Stillbirth and Neonatal Death Society) – 28 Portland Place, London W1N 4DE Tel: 020 7436 5881 email: support@uk-sands.org – A self-help organisation for parents bereaved by stillbirth.

Lesbian and Gay Bereavement Project – Vaughan M Williams Centre, Colindale Hospital, London NW9 5HG Helpline: 020 8455 8894 every evening 7pm-12pm – Offers help to lesbians and gay people.

Miscarriage Association – c/o Clayton Hospital, Northgate, Wakefield, West Yorkshire WF1 3JS email: miscarriageassociation@care4free.net website: www.miscarriageassociation.org.uk – Offers support and information for women, their partners and families, before or after a miscarriage, ectopic pregnancy or pregnancy loss.

National Association of Widows – 48 Queen's Road, Coventry CV1 3EH Tel: 024 7663 4848 – Offers self-help and friendship for widows.

Roadpeace – PO Box 2579 London NW10 3PW Helpline: 020 8964 1021 email: info@roadpeace.org.uk website: www.roadpeace.org.uk - Support and information for those bereaved by road death.

SAMM (Support After Murder and Manslaughter) – Cranmer House, 39 Brixton Road, London SW9 6DZ Tel: 020 7735 3838 email: samm@victimsupport.org.uk website: www.samm.org.uk – Can give details of local support groups.

Scottish Cot Death Trust – Royal Hospital For Sick Children, Yorkhill, Glasgow G3 8SJ Tel: 0141 357 3946 email: hblw@clinmed.gla.ac.uk - Offers an information and befriending network for families bereaved by an unexpected infant death.

Sudden Death Support Association – Dolphin House, Part Lane, Swallowfield, Reading, Berkshire RE7 1TB Tel: 01189 889797 – Offers a network for those who have lost someone through a sudden, accidental death, and puts people in touch with others who have suffered a similar bereavement.

Twin and Multiple Birthe Association – Bereavement Support Group - Harnott House, 309 Chester Road, Little Sutton, Ellesmere Port CH66 1QQ Helpline: 01732 868000 weekdays 7pm-11pm, weekends 10am-11pm email: enquiries@tambahq.org.uk website: www.tamba.org.uk – Offers support to those who lose a twin either at birth or later.

Victim Support – Cranmer House, 39 Brixton Road, London SW9 6DZ Helpline: 0845 30 30 900 9am-9pm email: contact@victimsupport.org.uk website: www.victimsupport.org - Offers contact details of local groups for people who have been the victim of crime.

Way Foundation – PO Box 74, Penarth, CF64 5ZD Tel: 029 2071 1209 email: info@wayfoundation.org.uk website: www.wayfoundation.org.uk – Offers self-help support and social activities for those widowed under the age of 50, and their children.

Youth Access – 2 Taylor's Yard, 67 Alderbrook Road, London SW12 8AD Tel: 020 8772 9900 – Offers advice on counselling and advisory services for young people.

Literature

There is an increasingly wide range of books and booklets being produced on bereavement, and many of these include personal accounts of loss. Sometimes it can help us understand the emotions we are experiencing if we read of others and how they have coped with a similar bereavement.

Local libraries and bookshops may be a useful starting point and bereavement organisations can often recommend reading material.

Through Grief, Elizabeth Collick (Darton Longman & Todd). The author is a widow and also has many years experience as a bereavement counsellor.

A Grief Observed, C. S. Lewis (Fabor). Written in the months following the death of the author's wife.

When Bad Things Happen To Good People, Harold Kushner (Pan). A universal question explored with great sensitivity by the author after the death of his son.

'When our Baby Died' - Video with companion booklet *Grieving after the death of your baby* by Jenni Thomas, Nancy Kohner, and Bradbury Williams (Child Bereavement Trust). Bereaved parents speak about their experience of losing a child.

When Parents Die, Rebecca Abrams (Lette Self Support Series). The author offers support based on her personal experience and that of other bereaved young people.

A Very Easy Death, Simone de Beauvoir (Penguin). This famous French author writes about her dying mother.

How It Feels When A Parent Dies, ed J. Krementz (Gollancz). Children in the middle and teenage years talk about their feelings and how other people helped them.

A Special Scar, Alison Werthiemer (Routledge). The author lost her sister through suicide and explores the experiences of other people bereaved by suicide.

All In The End Is Harvest- An Anthology For Those That Grieve, ed Agnes Whittaker (Darton Longman & Todd and Cruse).

HELP FROM THE DOCTOR

"I won't go and see my doctor, he'll only give me pills."
    "My doctor's always so busy. I don't want to waste his time."
    "What can a doctor do anyway?"
    Grief is not an illness. To be bereaved doesn't mean we have been made ill. There may be no reason necessarily for someone who has lost the person they love to visit their doctor. However, a good GP can be an invaluable source of support and information to a bereaved person.

Helpful and Non-Helpful Drugs
In old movies, the doctor's role when a death occurred in a family was clearly defined. He (generally it was a 'he') was called to the bedside of the shocked and grieving person and would administer something to make her sleep; and promise to pop in and see the patient again tomorrow.

Sleeping Pills
There is a growing recognition amongst the medical profession that sleep is not the answer to the pain of grief. Drugs - such as sedatives and tranquillisers - should be used only where there is a clear need for them, and then only for a limited period, with careful monitoring of any side effects.

    It is possible to get thoroughly run down in the early months of bereavement because of that combination of stress, anxiety and lack of sleep. At such a time it might be advantageous to have a drug administered which allows the body a chance to rest and recuperate a little, before once again taking up the hard work of grief. The situation where Grandma was put on sleeping pills after Grandad died, and is still unable to sleep without them twenty years later is rapidly becoming a thing of the past.

Anti-Depressants

If the normal depressed condition associated with bereavement becomes locked into a deeper depression sapping our internal coping mechanisms, then it might be wise to consult a doctor- who may well prescribe a course of anti-depressants. If at all worried about taking a prescribed drug it is sensible to discuss this with the doctor.

Using Our Doctor as a Source of Knowledge and Support

A good doctor is a valuable resource after a major bereavement. A doctor should have knowledge of grief, and will be able to distinguish natural grief and sadness from a deeper depression which requires treatment. They will be able to offer reassurance as to the normality of a wide range of intensely experienced feelings at this time. They will be able to monitor health. This is so often under attack in the early months of loss. Whilst grief itself isn't an illness, our health is vulnerable at this time due to the stress, and we do become more likely to fall prey to a whole range of bugs and diseases. Also, previous health problems may be reactivated. The doctor will take the symptoms we present seriously, and run any necessary tests before feeding that expert knowledge back to us. This can decrease the fear and anxiety we may be experiencing over our health.

If necessary, the doctor may be able to refer us on to another source of support; perhaps a local counselling service, or put us in touch with one of the many self-support groups now operating in this country, and where we might have the opportunity to meet others in a similar situation to ourselves.

Doctors cannot take our grief away from us. They are not magicians, and there is no cure for grief. Neither is there a 'correct way' of grieving the loss of someone we love. There are, however, basic steps we can take to ensure that we remain reasonably healthy. A good doctor is a valuable partner in this task.

Loss of Confidence in Our Doctor

Sometimes it can be hard to feel easy with a doctor who may also have treated the person we have lost. We may perhaps feel - genuinely or not - that the treatment was inadequate, or even that the doctor was guilty of neglect or made a wrong diagnosis. Such angry feelings and loss of confidence interferes with the relationship of trust which is essential if good doctoring is to take place. The alternatives are either to directly confront the doctor with these thoughts, or, if that is not possible, find another doctor.

Knowing that our doctor knows our parents or treats other close family members can be a barrier to discussing personal matters, especially if we suspect that what we say might be passed back to our family. However, before deciding to change doctors, it is sensible to give the matter careful thought; there are advantages in being with a doctor who knows us and our medical history.

Using Our Doctor

Doctors only have a short period of time to listen to our problems, make a diagnosis and suggest possible treatment. The average consultation period lasts for six minutes; therefore it is essential that we use this time to our best advantage.

"Fine" is not the best response to our doctor's query about how we are feeling. Obviously we are not totally fine - or we wouldn't be in the surgery.

It is a good idea to work out in advance what is worrying us, and if necessary, write the problems down on a piece of paper; starting with the most important one - the one which we are most anxious about.

Many people emerge from the doctor's surgery clutching a prescription, but having failed to mention the fact that they are really worried about their head, or the pain in their chest, or back, or stomach.

Describe symptoms carefully and clearly; doctors are not magicians. They are incapable of making a proper diagnosis unless we tell them how we feel.

If the doctor seems to be on the wrong track, pluck up courage and tell him so - further information might nudge him in the right direction!

Don't be afraid to ask for tests. Some may be unnecessary, but there can be an enormous relief in knowing that we do not have various diseases. After a major bereavement we can be particularly anxious over our health. This is natural. After all, we have been close to death and this will have affected our outlook on life.

If symptoms persist do go back to the doctor. Sometimes a series of visits is needed before a complaint is successfully diagnosed and treated.

Student Medicine

Some universities and colleges have doctors attached, others provide a list of those working in the vicinity. Before joining a doctor's list, it is sensible to first make a few enquiries from colleagues or neighbours to see what they think of their doctor. Joining a health unit where there is the option to see several doctors gives a wider choice, but there are also obvious advantages in seeing the same doctor each time.

In emergencies, we can ask to be seen by any doctor. Advice and help can also be obtained from the casualty department of one's local hospital.

Knowing one's National Health number can be useful. A new doctor will need this for registration.

Psychiatrists

Occasionally, a doctor will recommend that a patient sees a psychiatrist. This does not mean that one is mad or seriously disturbed. Psychiatrists are doctors who specialise in mental health and illness. Psychiatrists will diagnose the problem, and recommend a course of action; they might offer access to group counselling, or therapy. A few will provide counsel themselves. They often recommend a course of drugs.

COUNSELLING HELP

There are many different kinds of counsellors in this country. The help they offer ranges from the long-term psycho-therapeutic approach, where one is encouraged to talk over problems in depth; to the short-term behavioural contract with a therapist who will concentrate on working on specific problems (such as phobias) in a very practical way.

Most counsellors will have had a basic counselling training. They will have been taught to listen carefully, to concentrate on what is being said to them and to think clearly. They should have the ability to help the person they are working with express their thoughts and feelings in a safe environment. In doing so, the client is enabled to reach their own decisions about their life, and work through the problems they are confronting.

The safely of the counselling situation is partly created by the limitations of the relationship. A counsellor is not a friend, and so no friendship can be lost - whatever is said or left unsaid. There is no need for equality of need in counselling sessions. One does not expect to have to listen to one's counsellor describing the bad time he or she is having at the moment. The concentration of the sessions is focused on the client.

At its simplest level, counselling offers time to talk out difficult feelings in a safe place with a skilled listener.

Bereavement Counselling Help

If we have recently lost someone through death, then it may be most appropriate to talk with a bereavement counsellor. Alongside their basic counselling skills, they will have knowledge of the length and depth of grief, its variations and changing patterns.

Even if the death occurred some time ago there may be a wish to explore it once again at a later point in life.

The Citizen's Advice Bureaux should be able to supply details of the nearest Cruse branch, or other bereavement services.

Bereavement: A Catalyst

A bereavement can bring to the surface long-buried family difficulties or deep-rooted behavioural problems. Although bereaved, bereavement counselling would not be the most appropriate source of support for such a person in dealing with these intense feelings carried forward from the past. It may be better to use them as the basis for deeper self-investigation with a counsellor or therapist prepared to work with us helping us delve into our past history.

Other Kinds of Counselling Help

If there's no bereavement counselling service available in our area we may need to investigate other sources of counselling support. Counselling services specifically for young people exist in some parts.

Organisations such as Relate and the Westminster Pastoral Foundation offer skilled counselling throughout Great Britain. Many universities and colleges have their own counselling services, offering a valuable continuing link with a counsellor. Nearly all these sources of counselling support are available either free, or operate a sliding scale of payment dependent upon the client's ability to pay.

The Cost of Help

Private counselling or therapy can be very expensive. If thinking of undertaking long-term counselling, it is sensible to investigate thoroughly the differing kinds of help available. Such a financial investment in our own nature may be well worth the money if our problems are seriously interfering with our ability to live a good or fulfilling life. Most good therapists and counsellors will offer an initial diagnostic consultation; many operate on a sliding scale of payment.

The British Association for Counselling issues a list of accredited counsellors. Psychotherapists should have undertaken an extensive period of training at one of the recognised centres of psychotherapy.

Books Written By 'Experts' On Grief

Bereavement, studies of grief in adult life, Colin Murray Parkes (Penguin)

Anatomy of Bereavement, B. Raphael (Unwin Hyman) based on the author's research and work with those bereaved in different situations.

The Courage to Grieve, Judy Tatelbaum (Cedar). An experienced therapist writes simply and with understanding about many aspects of grief and mourning.

HELP FROM A MINISTER OF RELIGION

For the vast majority of people in this country, the death of someone they love will almost immediately bring them into direct contact with their particular place of worship. Usually a minister of religion will conduct the cremation or funeral ceremony.

Most religions play an important part in those 'rites of passage' which mark the major turning-points in life. Birth, marriage and death are seen as significant events requiring specific religious recognition.

Each religion acknowledges death in its own particular way, and the ceremonies surrounding the disposal of the body will reflect the importance each gives to those bereaved by the loss and to the particular belief in what happens after death.

In those confused and stunned early days of bereavement, it can be of immense comfort to place oneself and the care of the one we have lost into the hands of our particular church, synagogue or mosque. Ministers and religious leaders of all faiths are used to dealing with death. It is part of their life and their work. They are there to offer help and to guide us through this difficult and distressing time.

Life After Death

It may not be until we face our first major adult bereavement that we give serious thought to what happens after our death. At such a time we are challenged to examine our previous ideas and theories. Do we believe in a life after death? Will we meet up once more with the one we have lost? Is it possible to contact the dead through mediums and spiritualists?

We may also be searching for a greater understanding of the meaning and purpose to life itself. Why do we live? Why do some people die prematurely? How much control do we have over existence?

The Need to Question

The death of someone we love may lead us to question our belief in our God. How can we believe in a God that allows bad things to happen to good people? Why were our prayers unanswered?

Some people, in the early months following their bereavement, find that they have not only lost the person they love, but have also lost their trust in God and religion.

Such questioning is an important and very natural reaction to a great loss. It is through questioning that we are eventually able to move on towards a new understanding of our beliefs. It can help to have a skilled explorer of such thoughts alongside us at such a time.

Our priest, rabbi, minister or religious leader will have the knowledge necessary to guide us through this difficult process. If they have been working within their religious organisation for any length of time, they will frequently have confronted death, burial, cremation, and the pain and anguish of those bereaved through death.

The Religious Community

Being part of a community that worships together can make us feel loved and cared for and there can be great comfort in attending services and being made to feel that we matter and that our presence is required.

Perhaps there should be no safer place to express the feelings of grief and sadness than in this setting; for it is here that we might expect to be accepted just as we are.

Some people feel hesitant about attending services when they are in the process of questioning their beliefs. At a time when they need to be a part of the community it seems as if it too is denied to them.

Many religious leaders have had periods when they have questioned their beliefs. The fact that we are working through these important thoughts should not prevent us from gaining comfort from our community.

In Search of New Understanding

Some people find, in their search for understanding of the loss they have suffered and the effect it is having on their life, that other religions offer fresh insight. They come to believe other religious orders can give comfort and support at a time when it is most needed, and provide the companionship so longed for at this time of great loneliness

Unfortunately, there are some extreme cults and fringe religious movements that draw their following from young people who, for one reason or another, are vulnerable. These are recognisable because they seek to split and divide their followers from other religious groups and even from their friends and families.

We are at a point in history when most of the major religions are struggling to find a common ground between them. There are real attempts to emphasise the factors that join all religions together, rather than those which separate and divide them.

HELPING OURSELVES

Ultimately, grief cannot be shared with another person. Our feelings remain our feelings whether we talk about them or keep them private. Our pain is our pain, and our anger remains our anger.

Without any kind of specialist help most of us will find our own way through our own grief and learn to live successfully once again.

If the pain is too great, we, very sensibly, create our personal defences which protect us until we become strong enough to cope. Eventually, our feelings will find a way through to the surface, and we will find a way of dealing with them.

Listening to Ourselves
The loss of someone we love is a major turning-point in our life. It deserves attention, and we who are going through that loss deserve to give ourselves all the attention, the dignity, and the time we may need, to rebuild our life and learn to live without the one we have lost. Perhaps the best way we can help ourselves is by listening carefully to what our senses are telling us.

If our body is exhausted and pleading for a rest then why not allow it a space to do just that and plan an early night. Perhaps our work load is simply too great at the moment. If so, we might need to think seriously about how it can be reduced. Could we drop our hours at work until we feel stronger? The alternative might be illness and no work at all for a while.

What tasks in the home can be put to one side? Would someone be able to dig the garden for us or have the children for an evening so that we could go out or just be alone with our thoughts for a few hours?

Is our body getting over-tired because we are not looking after it? Even if we don't feel like eating we still need food to give us energy. Even if we can't sleep at night we still need regular periods of rest.

Burying oneself under a mountain of work can be a way of coping with the pain and sadness. If we do feel guilty about something we did or failed to do in the past then not looking after our body is a kind punishment. No-one benefits from this. It does not bring back the dead person, it creates anxiety for our friends and family, and leaves us weak and exposed to illness at a time when we most need all our strength for the intensely hard and painful work of grief.

When we are feeling low or unhappy it is important that we give ourselves the comfort we need. This is especially true if it is the person who used to comfort us that we have lost. If we succeeded in a particular task then we fully deserve a reward. If we feel in need of help then it's sensible to investigate what support is on offer in our particular area.

We may have to be patient with ourselves for grief can hit us hard and affect us for a long time. There is an old saying - Charity begins at home. After a major bereavement our ability to care should definitely start with ourselves. For, if we cannot care for ourselves at this difficult time, it is unlikely we will be able to extend love and care to those around us. And if we do not see ourselves as worthy of care then why should our friends or family! We may feel lost and alone and have little belief in ourselves or in the future, but we still matter. There is a great deal of difference between this necessary concentration of resources on ourselves at a time when it is most needed, and being self-centred or self-pitying; two qualities that are usually frowned upon. If we give ourselves the help we need we will survive and not just survive, but ultimately find a way of using the knowledge and skills which that process of survival has forced us to develop.

Moving On

Ultimately the greatest honour we can do those we love who have died is to take the best of what they gave us and carry it forward into our future with respect and appreciation. If we are monitoring ourselves carefully then we will recognise when we reach the point where we need to give ourselves permission to move forward, away from the past and our grief; a time when it is right to take on new responsibilities, make new relationships and create the new future that belongs to us and us alone. To do so is not a denial of the importance of the person who died but rather a celebration of their life and of the rich inheritance of learning, thoughts and memories they gave us.